Resurrecting Bertha

Buying back our wedding car
after 26 years in storage

ROB SIEGEL

Photo by Brian Ach.

HACK MECHANIC PRESS

Resurrecting Bertha: Buying back our wedding car after 26 years in storage

By Rob Siegel

Copyright ©2019 by Rob Siegel

All rights reserved. No part of this book may be used or reproduced in any manner whatsoever without written permission from the publisher, except for brief quotations in critical articles and reviews.

ISBN: 978-0-9989507-2-3

Library of Congress Control Number: 2019911385

The author and publisher recognize that some words, model names, and designations mentioned in this book are the property of the trademark holders. They are used only for identification purposes.

Portions of this work appeared previously in *Bimmerlife* and are reprinted here with permission of the BMW Car Club of America (BMW CCA) where applicable.

This is not a repair manual. The author is not a professional mechanic. Neither the author nor the publisher are responsible if you injure yourself while working on or driving your car. If you have any doubt as to your ability to do some of the things described in the book, or as to whether your car is safe to drive after doing them, don't do them, and seek the services of a professional mechanic instead.

Photographs by Rob Siegel except where noted
Design by King+Sons

Printed in the United States

The Hack Mechanic™ is a registered trademark of Rob Siegel

Hack Mechanic Press
19 Mague Place
West Newton, MA 02465

hackmechanicpress.com

Acknowledgements

To Maire Anne, who tolerates as much as you think, but more than you can possibly know.

To the BMW Car Club of America (BMW CCA) and *Roundel* magazine, for 34 years of community.

To Scott Sturdy and his volunteer support staff at The Vintage—the best BMW party around.

To Paul Wegweiser, you magnificent crazy fuck.

To Eric King who did the book design, and to Bruce Machon and Ed MacVaugh who proofread the draft and final versions.

But mostly to my mother, Bernice Siegel, to whom I owe all that I am.

Contents

Introduction 7

Part 1: The Repurchase 15

    The Origin Story: Me, Maire Anne, Bertha, and Alex 17

    What Did I Just Do? 39

    Dealing with the Crap 45

    Rolling the Stone Away 49

    Le Petite Resurrection 55

    The Great Escape 61

Part 2: Le Grande Resurrection 71

    The Decapitation 73

    The Glorious Failure 89

    Barely Drivable 105

    (43 Years Old And) Barely Legal 113

    Sorting the Charging System 131

    Getting Bertha Cold 139

    Fear of Flying 153

    The Clutch Performance 163

    The Facelift and Butt Tuck 171

    Adding Up the Costs 185

Part 3: Life After Resurrection 191
    Garage Space, Revisited 193
    The Fate of Bertha 199
    Vintage Prep 207
    The Road Trip 229
    The Wegweiserization 235
    Repairing the World, One Giubo at a Time 253
    Wrapping Up the Road Trip 261
Epilogue 265
My Mother Totally Deserves The Last Word 267
End Notes 269

Introduction

There are normal people. And then there are car people. Normal people regard cars as little more than appliances. They may experience a brief Subaru-commercial-like-pang when they sell their car and recall, with proper soft cinematic haze and thematic music, bringing a child home from the hospital in it, or a kid driving off in it to their prom, but overall, when the car is traded in for something bigger and safer and quieter, that's it. It's done. It's over. Meet the new boss, same as the old boss. The car isn't pined for any more than a broken toaster oven or a dishwasher is.

But to car people, it's different. Cars mean something to us. Sure, there are memories layered on top of our relationships with cars, but *the relationship itself* is a real thing, and the cars themselves are objects of passion and desire. We pour our time, our money, and our choices—that is, we pour *ourselves*—into them. The cars, bone stock or wildly modified, maintained on a shoestring budget or treated to an open-checkbook restoration, become a reflection of us. Hell, in many ways, they *are* us. It's no wonder we become so attached to them.

In the final chapter of my first book, *Memoirs of a Hack Mechanic,* I talk about the connection that many people feel to their old cars. We often remember them fondly, the way we do old lovers. But, as with an old lover, if you and a car drifted apart, there's usually a good reason. Everything has its time and place, and cars, even ones that we love, get old and get sold. Typically a car starts off as a daily driver. Perhaps, after a few years, it begins rusting. Perhaps it becomes unreliable. Perhaps our family needs dictate something newer, larger, and safer. Often it's a combination of all of these factors. Even if we love a car, if it's no longer filling its role, something else needs to take its place. While it *could* become a pampered enthusiast car, young people typically don't have the resources to build a garage or rent storage space to house a car they love as it transitions from daily driver to weekend warrior. Instead, we shed a tear and sell our old friend. It's ironic that, 20 years later and with more disposable income and garage space, many people try to recapture the magic by buying another example of that same car, but that seems to be the big ineluctable cycle of things.

As the vintage cars we once owned become valuable, many of us kick ourselves for selling what is now not only the rekindled object of our passion, but also an appreciating financial entity. "If only I had kept that car," we say to ourselves. "I loved that thing. And look at what they're bringing now. Why did I ever sell it? *How could I have been so stupid?*"

Fear not. Dry your tears. You're not stupid. (Well, probably not. I mean, I don't actually know you.) There is a rational explanation to this: The value of a car is only obvious after it has begun to go up. None of us have a crystal ball. Barrett-Jackson sold a 1965 21-window VW bus in 2017 for *three hundred thousand dollars*. Go ahead and tell me with a straight face you would've predicted *that*.

And even if you did, it probably wouldn't have mattered, because when you're young and need a new (or newer) car, you need to sell the old one to make way for it because you lack both the money and the space. If you're lucky, you have room for one daily driver for you and one for your spouse. Owning a third lightly-driven car becomes a nontrivial expense in terms of footprint, annual registration, inspection, taxes, and insurance, not to mention maintenance.

And let's be candid, the biggest expense isn't really "maintenance," it's that *you keep fucking with the car*. You decide it needs the correct original alloy wheels—no, scratch that, original alloys are so 2008; it needs the correct original *steel* wheels and hubcaps. Or that it's showing too much wheel well and it needs lowering springs to settle it down an inch and a half. Or, even if it's running fine, you want to try that new 123 distributor because everyone on bmw2002faq.com says they're the shiznit. If the car is within groping range, you're going to keep doing this, and it's going to keep sucking money.

So, mothball it, right? If you have the space, sure, you can store the car, but even if you're blessed with a two-car garage, the car begins competing for valuable real estate with its functional brethren and sistren and the bicycles and the lawnmower and the snow blower and the other stuff of life. If you're short on space like most people are, in theory, sure, you can rent storage somewhere and let the car silently appreciate in value, but in practice, it gets wicked pricey wicked fast. Very few of us have the financial resources to pay for decades of external storage.

The math is easy. In suburban Boston, renting half of someone's two-car garage costs about $300/month. That's $3,600 per year, or $36,000 for ten years of storage. And that's not 24-hour access garage space; they typically want you to roll the car in around Thanksgiving and out over Memorial Day weekend. Even if you find bargain-rate space for half that, you're still looking at a very big bill. Are you *that* sure of the car's appreciating value? No? I didn't think so. That's why so few people do it.

This calculus also helps explain the number of "barn-find" cars. If you have a car you can't afford to keep on the road but hate to sell, and know someone with a barn on their property you can use, the barn, even with the leaky roof and the rodents and spiders and all, starts to look pretty good.

In contrast, if you're a wealthy collector, you probably already have either a dual-use building—some warehouse associated with your business in which you also keep cars—or a dedicated outbuilding to house your collection. In either case, the incremental cost of storing each additional car is negligible. Sucks to be rich, right? Add enthusiast car storage to the list of things rich people can do that most of us mere financial mortals can't.

So, for all these reasons, most of the time, when a car's time as a daily driver is over, we just suck it up and sell it.

It's normal to feel a sense of loss for a car you loved and to wonder where it is. Many people are surprised to learn that, in Neil Young's song "Long May You Run," he's not singing about a girl—he's singing about his 1948 Buick hearse. In the last verse, he wonders if the Beach Boys are using it to ferry surfers and boards. I still frequently have dreams about the 1970 Triumph GT6+ I bought after graduating high school in 1976 and sold my junior year of college in 1978. In the dream, I usually find that the GT6 is still sitting in my mother's carport in Amherst, with the dream-logic—the same kind that causes dead relatives to appear with the dream-sensible explanation that there was simply a mistake—being that the buyer never picked it up. The odds that this particular car, which was rusty the day I bought it, survived to the present is extremely remote. I wouldn't want it back anyway. It was a miserable piece of British garbage, one that warned me off Brit bits until I bought the dead-since-1979 Lotus Europa Twin Cam Special, which is, as they say, another story. I also still dream about the 1969 Plymouth Satellite on which I learned to drive, and the '63 Rambler Classic that my friend John sold me for a dollar after he got married and his parents bought him and his wife a real car.

Figure 1: My 1970 Triumph GT6+. Garbage, but memorable enough to still dream about. Photo by Doug Weston.

Now, there *is*, in fact, a car I never should've sold—my 1982 Porsche 911SC. It was Rosewood (metallic brown), a Targa with a whale tail, making it more than a little bit garish and boy-racer-ish. I didn't care. I just loved it. I loved the flawless seating and steering wheel position. I loved the way you could hear the 12 quarts of oil gurgle. I loved how the steering wheel fought you when you cornered due to the centering force created by the front end's positive caster. I loved how the removable Targa top was nearly as good at giving you that open-sky experience as a convertible. I loved how every 14-year-old boy who saw it would say "oh, man, that thing is *awesome!*"

I didn't buy the SC as an "asset." I bought it because I always wanted a 911, and the SC was the one that made sense and that I could afford. It slotted perfectly between the small-bumpered long-hood 911s which already were going for big money, and the newer cars that hadn't yet hit the bottom of the depreciation curve. I owned it for ten years, and had very little trouble with it. It was everything a 911SC is supposed to be—a largely bullet-proof 911 with the bugs worked out of it, new enough to have a galvanized body but old enough to be free of electronic nannies. I daily-drove it until it was 25 years old, at which point it was eligible to go on my Hagerty policy. This dropped the insurance down to a fraction of what I'd been paying, but as with any car insured on an "agreed-value" policy, I could no longer daily-drive it, and had to keep it in a locked garage. Fortunately, I worked in an industrial building that had space not only for the SC, but also for my 635CSi and a ratty 2002 I'd picked up.

Then, in the early 2010s, my long-time engineering job began to wobble. The building where I worked and stored the three cars rent-free was abruptly closed, and I thought I was going to get laid off. I had to make some painful decisions. At the time, I owned seven cars. Clearly the three in the warehouse needed to go. I'd look at the 911SC and, in my mind, I'd see a cartoon balloon over it, with the car saying "I am frivolous and worth four mortgage payments." I sold the SC for what I paid for it — ten grand. And this was no panicked sale; I had it on eBay and Craigslist. Local 911 guys came and looked at it. With 140k on it, oil that was starting to get sucked past the valve guides, and a rust blister forming on the passenger door, ten grand was what the car was worth.

Figure 2: The car I never should've sold: The '82 911SC Targa with a tail.

At the time, I thought I did great with the SC. I bought it for ten grand. I owned it for ten years. I sold it for ten grand. There was an almost cosmic symmetry about it. Plus, SCs and Carreras (3.0 and 3.2 liter 911s) were commodities. They didn't rust like the older small-bumpered long-hood 911s, so their supply wasn't self-reducing. And they were sold in sufficient quantity that I thought they wouldn't go nuts like the earlier 911s. I thought that, when my job situation stabilized and I found other storage space, I'd spend, say, eighteen grand and buy a late 80s Carrera with a G50 transmission and hydraulic clutch.

But then, I didn't lose my job. While I was glad for that, about three months after I sold the SC, the prices on *all* air-cooled Porsches went nuts. SC and Carrera prices skyrocketed. As of this writing, I doubt I could buy that car back for thirty grand. It was especially sad because the car had already transitioned out of the needs-to-be-a-reliable-daily-driver-or-else-it-gets-sold hot seat; it was on my Hagerty policy and had storage space allocated to it. By my own narrative above, it should've been safe. But I let it slip away. It's my big automotive regret. I never should've sold it.

And yet, when I look back at it, I don't know how I could've made any other decision. The sword of Damocles was hanging over my head. I thought I was going to lose my job, and I *did* lose my free storage space. I owned an unsupportable number of frivolous vehicles. Lack of money and space are irresistible forces, and cars are the very essence of movable objects.

But, oddly, although I kick myself for the poor timing of selling the SC, I don't really pine for it as much as you'd think, either the model or that specific one I owned. Perhaps it was that I owned it far enough into middle age that the experiences I had in and with the car just weren't significant enough. There were no all-night gonzo runs in the SC, no wild contorted uncomfortable sex in it, both of which peppered my time with the GT6 (just sayin'). Come to think of it, there wasn't even a road trip. These are the things that create memories and intimacy. I largely just commuted to work in it, and when it went on the Hagerty policy, drove it around on the weekends. Not exactly activities that sear a car into the soul.

(Actually, I *do* have one particularly intimate memory of the SC. I was reasoning through the issues behind selling it and decided to take it for a drive and see how it felt. I came into the exit ramp off I90 to Rt 16 in West Newton near my house. It's a right-hander that for a short stretch goes off-camber. A combination of coming into it too hot, twelve-year-old rubber, and the classic don't-*ever*-do-that lifting off the throttle in mid-turn, brought the back end of the car around. I almost stuffed it into the guardrail. I took it as an omen and went through with the sale.)

Sheriff Johnson. Now *that* was a car—Maire Anne's 1971 VW bus, so-named because of a bumper sticker that came on the back. She bought it in 1979 when she was working in Cambridge but I was still in college in Amherst. I thought, how cool is this: My hot girlfriend just bought the car synonymous with road-tripping, reefer, and sex. In addition to all of the back-and-forth between Amherst and Cambridge, we did many jaunts up north to go hiking. There was one memorable New Year's excursion to The White Mountains where, the morning we left, it was negative twenty degrees out, and the Sheriff was the only car in the parking lot that started (well, I *did* warm up the oil pan with the Svea camping stove). We took it on a trip to a Rainbow Gathering in

West Virginia in 1980. That's what you're *supposed* to do in a VW bus.

When we moved to Austin in early 1982, we drove down in the Sheriff. My memories of that trip are forever intertwined with the car, including fixing it by the side of I-30 when the points closed up in Texarkana (it's *always* the fucking points).

Unfortunately, the Sheriff carried a bit too much of its New England heritage with it, because once we were down in Austin, it was rusty enough that a bottle jack went through one of the frame rails. I found a rust-free '69 Westfalia camper with a dead engine, yanked the engine out of the Sheriff, put it in the camper, and sold the Sheriff as a parts car. So the odds that the Sheriff survived are basically zero.

Figure 3: Sheriff Johnson (left) and the '69 camper (right) in the middle of the engine swap in Austin in 1983.

The Westfalia, with its fold-out bed, pop-top, stove, and icebox, was fun. Maire Anne and I camped a few times in it, but mainly it was just her car. It then moved up to Boston with us in '84. Maire Anne daily-drove it for years. Our band transported equipment to gigs in it. Then, our first child was born, at which point spreading rust, infant seat attachment issues, and general concerns about safety caused us to sell it. We let it go for $500. Yeah, I know, but we were living in Boston, I had two BMWs usurping both parking spaces in my incredibly tolerant mother's garage, and that's what it was worth at the time; what were we *supposed* to do with it? In many ways, selling the camper was the perfect microcosm of the issues involved with not being able to hold into a beloved car.

Some folks try and track down the actual car they wish they'd never sold. In this web-enabled world, it's amazing what you can find by just googling the VIN. I know people who have run the issue to ground and learned that their beloved car was scrapped. That's sad, but at least it's a definitive answer, like Fox Mulder finally learning what happened to his sister.

Whether you find your original car or settle for buying another example of the same model, maybe it works out, maybe it doesn't. Maybe it's like running into an old lover and wondering what you ever saw in them. Or maybe it's more like a Facebook relationship—a flush of excitement at the reconnection, a few messages recounting old times, and then it naturally runs its course, peters out, and you part ways a second time. It's tough. Once you take the rose-colored glasses off, old cars are creaky and fragrant. You have to love them a lot to live with them for the long haul. Having bailed out once, and gotten accustomed to newer cars, it's a lot to expect to pick up right where you left off. As both Thomas Wolfe and A.E. Housman said, you can't go home again.

Or maybe, just maybe, the spark is still there and the fire can be re-lit.

The purpose of this book to tell my story, in which I not only went home again, I pulled into the driveway in the same car.

And that brings us to Bertha.

Part 1

The Repurchase

The Origin Story: Me, Maire Anne, Bertha, and Alex

My fond memories of the Triumph GT6, the Porsche 911SC, and Maire Anne's VW bus and camper notwithstanding, I am primarily a vintage BMW guy, with a particular fondness for 2002s, the boxy little sedans built from 1968 through 1976. I imprinted on a round tail light 2002 when I was 13, owned by a Hampshire College student who lived with us for a summer, and I seem doomed to follow that model around for the rest of my life. When I was in college, I worked for that same fellow summers and winters. He'd graduated from the 2002 to a 733i 4-speed, which I got to errand-run all around Boston. The degree of solidity of that car, even at triple-digit speeds, was a revelation. I vowed that I would right the error I'd made with the GT6, and that my next car would be a BMW.

When Maire Anne and I moved down to Austin in 1982 and I began earning a bit of money, I finally bought my first BMW 2002. It was a '71, equal parts Colorado (orange), bondo, and surface rust, and had a whiny transmission, but I didn't care. It ran and drove. I paid $800. I was thrilled. When I got it home, I checked the transmission fluid and found that it was completely dry. I filled the transmission with fluid, took the car for a test drive, and grinned ear-to-ear when the whine was gone. A-*ha*, I thought, my first repair on a 2002 and I totally nailed it. Transmission fluid. Whine gone. Eight hundred bucks. Man, I frikkin' *stole* this thing.

The next morning, I found the transmission fluid all over the driveway. Because, of course, transmission fluid doesn't evaporate from a closed transmission. If it's gone, it's because it leaked out. In my case, it turned out that the transmission end cover was cracked where the shift lever went through it. No problem, I thought; I'll pull the transmission and replace the end cover. I then learned that these Getrag transmissions are constructed in such a way that the gear train is largely suspended from the end cover, essentially making the cover the case and the case the cover, and that you need special tools to even get to first base taking them apart.

So my first repair working on a BMW 2002 literally was rebuilding the transmission. If that's not a trial by fire for the start of a life-long relationship, I don't know what is.

I had the Colorado car repainted, and shortly after, found a Malaga (burgundy) '72 2002 that had something the '71 didn't—air conditioning. After all, this *was* Austin, and it *was* hot. I bought it and sold the Colorado car. This set up the pattern that remains to this day, except that I'm much better at buying cars than I am at selling the ones I already own.

Figure 4: My first (rear) and second (front) 2002s in Austin in 1983, and my only and very adorable wife.

Now, as any vintage BMW fan knows, the BMW 2002s built from 1968 through 1973 have round tail lights and small chrome bumpers, and those built from 1974 through 1976 have square tail lights and, on U.S.-spec cars, bumpers so big that they look like they're designed to protect wharfs from errant cruise ships. So it's perhaps surprising that, when Maire Anne's and my short sojourn in Austin was ending in 1984 (we enormously enjoyed our two and a half years there, but were going back to Boston to get married and put down roots near both of our families), I began actively looking for a big-bumpered 2002. But there *was* method to my madness: My theory was that a later big-bumpered car might stand a better chance in the demolition derby that is Boston traffic and parking. Nowadays, the pre-'74 2002s with the small chrome bumpers, perky round tail lights, and period-'70s interiors are iconic appreciating classics, whereas the big-bumpered cars, with their generic steering wheels, one-piece molded dashboards and rugs, faux wood-grained instrument clusters, and less-interesting pleated seat patterns, are, well, what you buy when you can't afford a roundie (it's cruel because it's true). But back in 1984, 2002s were still fairly recent cars that many people used as daily drivers, and the big-bumpered cars offered the additional advantage that they were simply newer, and thus were often less beat-up then their perkier cuter roundie counterparts.

After some searching, I found Bertha, a '75 2002 with working air conditioning. Her name originated from those bridge abutment bumpers, since with them, she was anything but dainty. In addition, the car's battleship gray paint looked like it had chunks of cement mixed into it. Bertha was never pretty, but she always looked purposeful.

I paid $2500 for the car. Actually, I didn't pay it; Maire Anne did. Actually, she didn't pay it either; she borrowed $2000 of it. We were in our mid-20s. Neither of us had $2500 in the bank. But she had an account with the University of Texas Credit Union. A few signed papers, a bank loan, and Bertha was mine. I mean hers. I mean ours. (Seriously, I mean mine.)

It never ceases to amaze me what pieces of memorabilia survive multiple moves, marriage, children, purges, etc. Remarkably, I still have Bertha's original dealer window sticker, the bill of sale, and Maire Anne's loan paperwork.

Now, another thing you need to know is that, almost uniformly across the automotive world, 1975 is the absolute worst model year for U.S.-spec cars. This is because emission control requirements that had been ratcheting up since 1968 underwent a step change. To comply with the new stricter tailpipe standards, most manufacturers installed catalytic converters in the middle of the exhaust, but BMW and a handful of other manufacturers instead used devices called thermal reactors. These injected air into the exhaust to increase the temperature, which in turn helped to oxidize CO and HC (unburned hydrocarbons) into CO_2 and H_2O. Unfortunately, the reactors were integrated directly into the exhaust manifold, which, in turn, was bolted directly to the head. The unit ran so hot that, at night, if you opened up the hood, you could see it glowing red. Because of this, thermal reactors were a disaster, often causing a car's head to crack.

So I now marvel at the fact that I sold a rust-free roundie and replaced it with not only a big-bumpered 2002, but arguably the *worst* big-bumpered 2002—a '75 with horrible levels of emission controls—but the reasons made sense to me at the time. Plus, I didn't keep the '75's engine in Bertha. I had just rebuilt the engine in the Malaga '72 car, so when I bought Bertha, I immediately swapped engines, putting the newly-rebuilt one in Bertha, and the '75 engine in the '72, then selling the '72. (And yes, when I put Bertha's engine in the '72, I replaced the thermal reactors with a conventional exhaust manifold.)

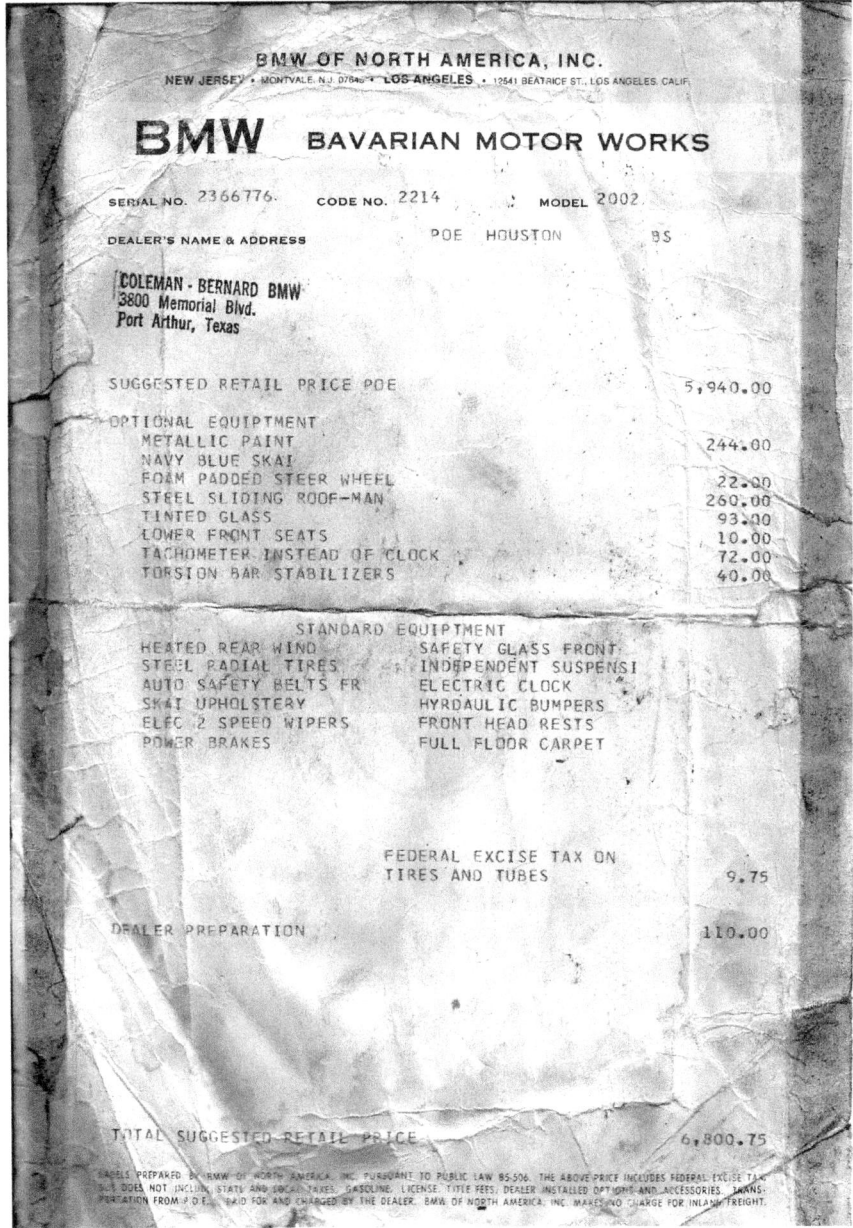

Figure 5: Bertha's original window sticker.

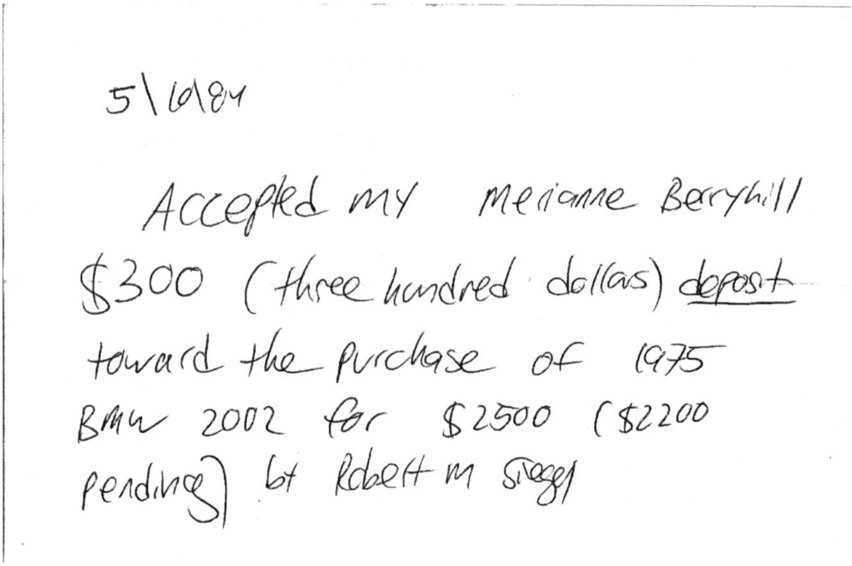

> 5\6\84
>
> Accepted by Merianne Berryhill
> $300 (three hundred dollars) ~~deposit~~
> toward the purchase of 1975
> BMW 2002 for $2500 ($2200
> pending) by Robert M Siegel

Figure 6: Bertha's bill of sale.

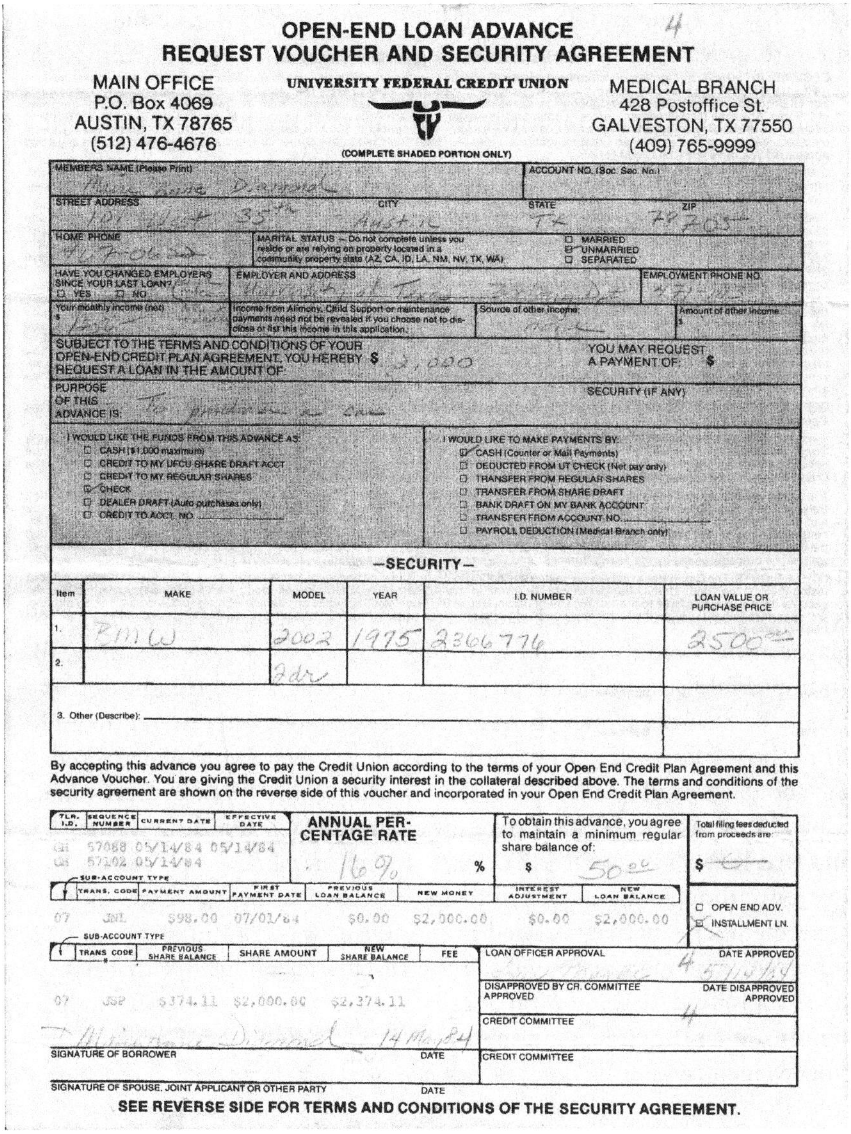

OPEN-END LOAN ADVANCE
REQUEST VOUCHER AND SECURITY AGREEMENT

MAIN OFFICE
P.O. Box 4069
AUSTIN, TX 78765
(512) 476-4676

UNIVERSITY FEDERAL CREDIT UNION

MEDICAL BRANCH
428 Postoffice St.
GALVESTON, TX 77550
(409) 765-9999

(COMPLETE SHADED PORTION ONLY)

MEMBERS NAME (Please Print) — ACCOUNT NO. (Soc. Sec. No.)
STREET ADDRESS — CITY — STATE — ZIP
HOME PHONE — MARITAL STATUS — Do not complete unless you reside or are relying on property located in a community property state (AZ, CA, ID, LA, NM, NV, TX, WA) — ☐ MARRIED ☒ UNMARRIED ☐ SEPARATED
HAVE YOU CHANGED EMPLOYERS SINCE YOUR LAST LOAN? ☐ YES ☐ NO — EMPLOYER AND ADDRESS — EMPLOYMENT PHONE NO.
Your monthly income (net) $ — Income from Alimony, Child Support or maintenance payments need not be revealed if you choose not to disclose or list this income in this application. — Source of other income: — Amount of other income $

SUBJECT TO THE TERMS AND CONDITIONS OF YOUR OPEN-END CREDIT PLAN AGREEMENT, YOU HEREBY REQUEST A LOAN IN THE AMOUNT OF $ 2,000 — YOU MAY REQUEST A PAYMENT OF: $

PURPOSE OF THIS ADVANCE IS: — SECURITY (IF ANY)

I WOULD LIKE THE FUNDS FROM THIS ADVANCE AS:
☐ CASH ($1,000 maximum)
☐ CREDIT TO MY UFCU SHARE DRAFT ACCT
☐ CREDIT TO MY REGULAR SHARES
☒ CHECK
☐ DEALER DRAFT (Auto purchases only)
☐ CREDIT TO ACCT. NO. ______

I WOULD LIKE TO MAKE PAYMENTS BY:
☒ CASH (Counter or Mail Payments)
☐ DEDUCTED FROM UT CHECK (Net pay only)
☐ TRANSFER FROM REGULAR SHARES
☐ TRANSFER FROM SHARE DRAFT
☐ BANK DRAFT ON MY BANK ACCOUNT
☐ TRANSFER FROM ACCOUNT NO. ______
☐ PAYROLL DEDUCTION (Medical Branch only)

—SECURITY—

Item	MAKE	MODEL	YEAR	I.D. NUMBER	LOAN VALUE OR PURCHASE PRICE
1.	BMW	2002	1975	2366776	2500
2.		2dr			
3. Other (Describe):					

By accepting this advance you agree to pay the Credit Union according to the terms of your Open End Credit Plan Agreement and this Advance Voucher. You are giving the Credit Union a security interest in the collateral described above. The terms and conditions of the security agreement are shown on the reverse side of this voucher and incorporated in your Open End Credit Plan Agreement.

TLR. I.D.	SEQUENCE NUMBER	CURRENT DATE	EFFECTIVE DATE
GH	57088	05/14/84	05/14/84
GH	57102	05/14/84	

ANNUAL PERCENTAGE RATE 16 %

To obtain this advance, you agree to maintain a minimum regular share balance of: $ 50.00

Total filing fees deducted from proceeds are: $ —

SUB-ACCOUNT TYPE	TRANS. CODE	PAYMENT AMOUNT	FIRST PAYMENT DATE	PREVIOUS LOAN BALANCE	NEW MONEY	INTEREST ADJUSTMENT	NEW LOAN BALANCE
07	JNL	$98.00	07/01/84	$0.00	$2,000.00	$0.00	$2,000.00

☐ OPEN END ADV.
☒ INSTALLMENT LN.

SUB-ACCOUNT TYPE	TRANS CODE	PREVIOUS SHARE BALANCE	SHARE AMOUNT	NEW SHARE BALANCE	FEE
07	JSP	$374.11	$2,000.00	$2,374.11	

LOAN OFFICER APPROVAL — DATE APPROVED
DISAPPROVED BY CR. COMMITTEE APPROVED — DATE DISAPPROVED APPROVED
CREDIT COMMITTEE
CREDIT COMMITTEE

SIGNATURE OF BORROWER — DATE 14 May 84
SIGNATURE OF SPOUSE, JOINT APPLICANT OR OTHER PARTY — DATE

SEE REVERSE SIDE FOR TERMS AND CONDITIONS OF THE SECURITY AGREEMENT.

Figure 7: Maire Anne's credit union loan agreement for Bertha.

As our return to Boston in August '84 neared, we had to figure out the logistics. That in and of itself was a story. A friend, Mike, who was also relocating north, came along, as did Maire Anne's sister Tricia. We wanted to take both Bertha and Maire Anne's '69 VW camper (why *wouldn't* you move two cool rust-free cars north?), plus all our stuff, including three cats. So we rented a U-Haul box truck and a tow dolly. Maire Anne and Tricia drove the camper, which gave the cats room to move around. And Mike and I drove the U-Haul, hauling Bertha behind us on a tow dolly. So as we left Austin and headed across Texarkana in August, the only car with air conditioning was the one being towed. It made sense, but it made no sense.

When we got back to Boston, Maire Anne and I moved into the 3rd floor of my mother's house in Brighton. We thought this would be temporary, but we wound up staying there for eight years. The house had a two-car garage that I instantly and completely usurped. My mother and sister were both incredibly tolerant of this. I put the half-axles back on Bertha (I'd removed them for the tow), and marveled that, for the first time, I was actually driving my own BMW around my home state. I felt like I'd not only arrived back home, but had done so as an adult.

As per the subtitle of this book, Maire Anne and I drove off in Bertha from our wedding on Labor Day 1984, the car covered in shaving cream and toilet paper, and with cans trailing from her massive rear bumper. At the time, I didn't really think about the car as being a player in the event. I mean it wasn't like the car was *in* the wedding, like an impossibly cute child or the family dog acting as the ring bearer. We simply drove my car, which was my nine-year-old daily driver, to and from the wedding. It wasn't until years later, when two couples asked me about borrowing a 2002 for their wedding, that I remembered that Maire Anne and I, in fact, drove off from our own wedding in a 2002, and that that 2002 was Bertha. I later found the photograph below. I've since thought about this in terms of what I said above about how we remember cars that we used in significant ways or did crazy-ass things in. Although now, with all the BMW-related history that has since transpired, driving off from our wedding in a 2002 seems highly significant, at the time, it wasn't in the least. It was either Bertha or the Volkswagen camper. *Those were just our cars.*

Figure 8: Our friends did a number on Bertha before Maire Anne and I drove off in it from our wedding. And yes, one of my classier friends did shaving-cream a dick on the side.

The next day, when we took Bertha to a car wash to get the shaving cream washed off, the attendant smiled and didn't charge us. "Wedding special," he said.

It is at this early juncture in my and Bertha's relationship that my friend Alex enters the picture. When he is asked how we met, Alex says: "Rob drove into my repair shop and asked if he could borrow a door." This is absolutely true. Shortly after the wedding, I'd damaged Bertha's driver's door backing the car out my mother's garage with the door ajar. I'd ordered another door, but when it arrived, it too was damaged. This was a problem, as Maire Anne and I had a honeymoon road trip planned, and I'd already taken Bertha's original dented door off. The vendor promised me a replacement for the door that was damaged in shipping, but it wouldn't arrive before we needed to leave. There was a repair shop across the street from my mother's house in Brighton called McCray's. I drove Bertha inside. A cheerful young man greeted me. "Can I help you?" he asked.

What I said was probably the last thing he ever imagined hearing: "Yes. I'd like to borrow a door."

"You want to… *borrow* a door?"

I explained what had happened, and how I had another door on the way, but it wouldn't arrive in time, thus justifying my entirely rational request to borrow a door. Alex did not *have* a door he could loan me, something I remind him of when *he* tells the story, lest he portray himself as more helpful in my door-related quest than he actually was. But it was, as they say, the start of a beautiful friendship. We spent years being 2002 buddies, wrenching together, and helping each other drive home and part out cars.

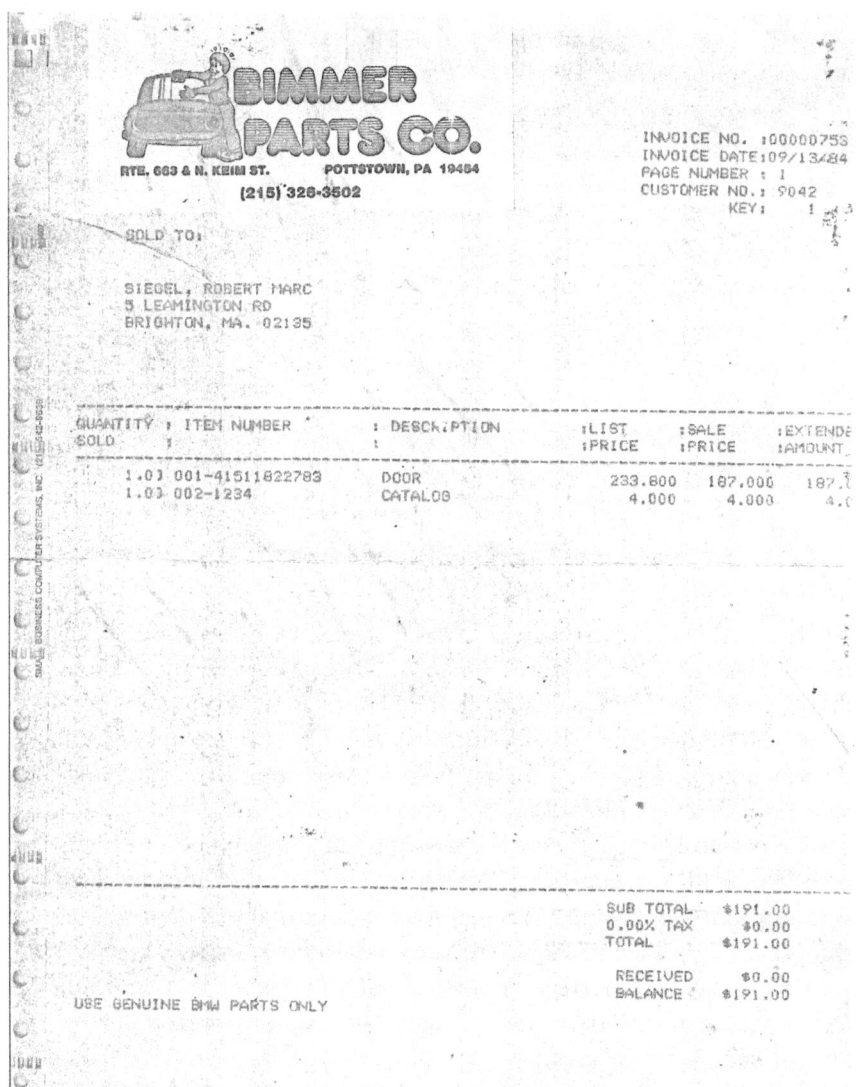

Figure 9: The receipt from Bimmerparts for Bertha's door.

Regarding my urgent need for a door, I wound up putting the old door back on Bertha so Maire Anne and I could take our honeymoon road trip. Then, when the new door arrived, I primed and installed it. I thought I'd soon get the whole car repainted, so I never bothered to put the trim back on the primed door.

Bertha became the vessel for my automotive dreams and the repository of a good deal of my disposable income. Over the years, she underwent a kind of transmogrification. There was the obligatory lusting after and purchasing of parts that were advertised in BMW CCA *Roundel* magazine. Despite my having installed the engine I'd just rebuilt in Austin, I had the persistent feeling that the car would be better if it had more power (real epiphany right there, huh?). I found a rusty '72 2002tii, my first of easily a dozen tiis that would follow. I instantly liked the power and the wind-up that the injection gives. I pulled its engine, put Bertha's engine in the tii, and used the tii as a winter beater. I then began rebuilding the tii engine to Euro spec with 10:1 pistons in preparation to drop it, Kugelfisher injection and all, into Bertha.

But in the middle of that process, I stumbled into a rotted 2002ti with a lunched engine. If you don't know, the 2002ti was the predecessor of the tii, with dual sidedraft carbs instead of injection. It was never commercially imported to the United States. 2002tis are now insanely rare, so this was the kind of car that if you were fortunate enough to stumble into now, you'd save it, but in 1986 it was just a rotted $250 parts car. I stripped it and put the dual Webers, big brake booster, master cylinder, front struts, big calipers, and rotors into Bertha, basically all the ti parts except the boxed rear A-arms and the clock, essentially turning Bertha into a big-bumpered ti tribute car. I even took the "2002ti" badge and put it on Bertha's butt.

Figure 10: The 2002ti parts car, stripped and waiting to be towed away as scrap, with Maire Anne in the background.

By the time I was done, Bertha read like she'd gone for a shopping spree in ten years' worth of 1980's *Roundel* magazine issues: 10:1 pistons, dual Weber 40DCOEs, 300 degree Iskenderian cam, Headercraft headers, Prima Flow exhaust, factory tropical radiator, Metric Mechanic gearbox, Koni suspension, Recaro interior (with that striped orange fabric that said "Recaro" on each of the seats like 12 times), Yokohama

A008 tires, auxiliary gauge cluster, Cibié Oscar driving lights, Wink mirror, killer stereo, on and on. When I took the car into Beaconwood Motors (who advertised on the back cover of *Roundel* for many years) to have the Webers jetted, they said it was one of the fastest 2002s they'd ever had in the shop. Perhaps transmogrification has to precede resurrection.

Not long after the engine rebuild and installation, I was driving Bertha when the battery light came on. I expected to find that the fan belt had snapped. When I opened the hood, I was surprised to see the belt still there. Puzzled, I fired the car back up. The battery light was still on. And the belt was stationary, which was, to say the least, odd, because the engine was still running. What the…? It took me a while to understand what I was seeing. The engine was running, but the crank pulley wasn't turning. It turned out that the Woodruff key holding the hub and crank pulley in place on the crankshaft had sheared off, and the hub was freewheeling on the front of the crank, ruining it. I had to pull the engine and replace the crank.

Thus, Bertha is the only car I've ever owned in which I rebuilt the engine, or at least portions of it, three times. And in a three-year period.

I daily-drove Bertha for the next seven years, swapping it for winter beaters when the roads got ugly. I took it to Boston CCA Chapter-sponsored track days at Lime Rock and the old NHIS Bryar track back when I used to do such things. And I began writing for *Roundel*, the magazine of the BMW Car Club of America. Many of my articles revolved around Bertha, either general 2002 pieces, nut-and-bolt repair articles, or discussing the pros and cons of a particular modification. These articles transitioned into my monthly column, *The Hack Mechanic,* which I still write today.

Then, in 1986, I bought my 1973 3.0CSi. It was a car that was rife with possibility, meaning it was a sexy E9 coupe cleverly disguised as a basket case. It had been hit in the front, and, despite a previous owner's ham-fisted attempts at bodywork, needed a nose and fenders. In addition, the glass and most of the interior were out of the car, and it barely ran. But I wanted an E9 more than nightly sex with Maire Anne (well okay maybe I wanted them the same amount), and this was the one I could afford. It's not that I abandoned 2002s, but Bertha's constant cycle of modification and improvement slowed considerably, as much of my temporal and financial resources were redirected at the lithe sexy but very needy E9 coupe.

Figure 11: My '73 3.0CSi after partial bodywork.

In 1987, when Maire Anne was pregnant with our first child, we took Bertha up to Cape Breton, Nova Scotia—our final road trip together before the kids were born. I vividly remember Maire Anne having apples and cheese and crackers at the ready on the 2002's dashboard at all times in case she got hungry (helpful hint to expectant fathers: when the expectant mother says she's hungry, it's not in your interest to make her wait). When we came back into the United States, customs agents at the border looked at the primer-painted door, suspicious that I was trying to illegally bring in a grey market car by deleting the VIN tag that should've been affixed to the original door. I showed them the VIN plate inside the engine compartment, and nervously explained about damaging the door backing out of my mother's garage—hell, I may have even babbled that I met this guy named Alex by asking if I could borrow a door. With the hood open, they looked *very* closely at the dual Webers, then pointed toward a fenced-in parking lot of confiscated high-dollar gray-market BMWs, Porsches, and Mercedes. Ultimately, the car *wasn't* a gray-market car, and I *did* already have it registered in Massachusetts, so they let me go.

Figure 12: Bertha on the ferry to Digby, Nova Scotia, in 1987.

Maire Anne and I were still living on the third floor of my mother's house in Brighton. It had two bedrooms, and the two-car garage that I'd usurped housed both Bertha and the E9 coupe. Our first child, Ethan, was born in 1988. Then, in 1990, our second child, Kyle, was born. As child #3 (human child, not car child) was approaching, we needed more space (human space, not car space; well, car space too). The house we bought in Newton in 1992 checked off the boxes of location, school system, and more room for the family, but ironically, it had less space for the cars. The 3.0CSi had just had an outer body restoration, including a new nose and fenders and seven coats of wet-sanded paint, and E9 coupes like the 3.0CSi are the kind of cars that will rust if you so much think a moist thought within 100 feet of them, so there was no question that it had dibs on the new house's single-car garage. This meant that, once we moved into the new house, Bertha would need to sit outside, a situation that would likely kill the car.

Around this time, Alex got married. Our band played at his wedding. His wife Heidi asked us to play a song she had written about how they'd met. It was to the tune of the old Sinatra standard "Strangers in the Night." She had me sing "Scoobie doobie doo… he had an old 2002… and it was *bluuuuue*." It was very sweet.

For their honeymoon, they were planning on taking Alex's blue 2002 on a big western road trip, doing "The Grand Circle" of national parks, but it needed some repairs. As their departure date neared, his car wasn't ready. I offered them use of Bertha—a well-sorted car with air conditioning—as a wedding present. Alex initially demurred—we are, after all, men, and we *don't* need help, thank you very much—but Heidi gently, and then not-so-gently, recommended that Alex take me up on my gracious offer. So off into the sunset they drove, not in a blue 2002, but in a gray one—Bertha.

When Alex and Heidi returned from their trip in Bertha six weeks later—a much longer road trip than Maire Anne and I had ever taken in the car— they and Bertha had bonded. We talked about my impending lack of garage space, and over the next few weeks, a deal was struck, and Alex bought Bertha. (Alex jokes "Yeah, we borrowed the car to go on our honeymoon, and never returned it.")

It was now seven years after Alex and I had first met because I drove Bertha, sans driver's door, into his shop and asked if I could borrow a door. Her replacement door was still in primer, and still had no trim on it.

[Above, I tell the story the way I've been telling it for years. In carefully reconstructing the dates for this book, however, it turns out that I didn't remember this part of the story the way it actually happened. When I say "It was now seven years since Alex and I had first met," that's wrong. It was four. This is because I've been incorrectly tying Bertha's sale to having more kids, moving out of Brighton, and buying the house in Newton with the one-car garage. Even though I remember it that way, it turns out that that timeline isn't possible. Alex and Heidi actually got married years before we began house-hunting. Maire Anne and I attended their wedding. Ethan was a baby. We have photos of him wearing a little infant onesie tuxedo. There's zero question that it was the summer of 1988. So there's zero question that Alex and Heidi's road trip in Bertha was the fall of 1988, after which I never got the car back from Alex. Alex confirms this. We bought the house in Newton not in 1988, but in the spring of 1992. So this isn't a small discrepancy—it's three and a half years. So why, exactly, did I sell Bertha when we were still living at my mother's house? Perhaps my mother and sister were less tolerant of my flagrant usurpation of both garage spaces than I remember, and gently pressured me into surrendering one of them. That's reasonable, but I clearly recall other BMWs coming and going while in Brighton. There are a few other possibilities. The first is that I was so strategic about the anticipated space needs that I foresaw and acted on them three and a half years out. I find this, shall we say, unlikely. The second is that the 3.0's needs were sucking me dry, and I sold Bertha for the money. This is plausible, but unlikely, as Alex paid me for Bertha half up front and half in installments. The third is that, having turned Bertha into a track rat, I grew tired of the way it felt as a daily driver. I know that this is a true statement, but I have no recollection of it being the main reason for the sale of the car. Of course it's possible that it was a combination of all of these factors, which is exactly the kind of thing likely to make the memory hazy. Why I'm so squishy on this but remember so many of the details of Bertha's three engine rebuilds… well, as they said repeatedly in *Shakespeare in Love*, "It's a mystery."]

Figure 13: Alex posing with Bertha in about 1990.

Alex had big plans for the car, including finally stripping off its cement-like finish, repainting it, door and all, and installing Euro bumpers (Alex was an early fan of the Euro "small-bumpered squarie" look before it became cool). I thought I had engineered a smooth transition that would ensure Bertha's safe future.

It's significant, at least to me, to note that not only was Bertha the first 2002 I owned as I returned to Boston in 1984 and joined the BMW CCA, it was also my *last* 2002 for nearly 15 years. Since the Newton house's one-car garage had to shelter the 3.0CSi, any other car I owned needed to sit outside. A parade of E12s, E28s, E30s, and E36s came and went as daily drivers, but it wasn't until my new garage was built in 2005 that I bought another 2002. So Bertha's sale, although I didn't know it at the time, was quite a bellwether event.

Unfortunately, after Alex bought Bertha, her fortunes went downhill. Alex got out of the BMW parts business and became a building contractor. His garage soon became occupied by tools and supplies, so Bertha was forced to sit on the Boston streets. This was the late '80s and early '90s when BMW stood for "Break My Window." The car was stolen and vandalized. It was recovered, and I fixed it after Alex and towed it back to my house with a rope. (Ah, youth.) As part of that work, Alex treated himself to a Getrag 245 5-speed transmission, which, as a birthday present, I installed for him. (I recall that I called up Jim Rowe at The Metric Mechanic and said "Send me whatever I need to install a 245 5-speed in a 2002." Ah, disposable income.)

But soon after, Bertha was stolen and recovered a second time. This time it came back more badly damaged: The front bumper was askew, the right front fender was dented, the right rear quarter panel was slightly pushed in, and the car was running badly enough that Alex suspected engine damage, like a floated valve from over-revving the motor. Sometime in 1991, Alex put Bertha in an unused and difficult to access garage located in the back of his neighbor's house. And there she sat, like the one true ring in *Lord of the Rings*, passing out of time, but not quite out of memory.

Decades flew by. Alex and I remained close. He built the kitchen and 3rd floor addition onto our house in 1995. And, in a remarkable bit of synergy between contracting and automotive worlds, he built my new garage in 2005.

The sheetrock wasn't even up on the walls of the new garage before I began buying 2002s again. The first one was a '73 tii that had just been repainted. The seller had gotten into a dispute with the bodyshop over a paint drip on the rear quarter panel. He pulled the car out of the shop and it sat, partially disassembled, in his garage in western Massachusetts. He eventually lost interest and sold it. I bought it and reassembled it. The first time I drove it, it instantly all came back. The big greenhouse of windows. The flawlessly sparse German interior. The great snickety feel of the gearshift and the directional. The crisp handling. And those perky round tail lights. Anyone who said you can't go home again never owned a 2002.

But with Alex's busy schedule, he never got back to *his* 2002—Bertha. She sat in his neighbor's garage for the next 26 years.

Busy people with multiple projects deal with them in a variety of ways. I am, above most things, a very practical person, with a good track record of not biting off more than I can chew (except for The Lotus Europa Of Which We Shall Not Speak). Alex, on the other hand, is a visionary who can picture in his head how he wants a finished project to look, but doesn't always get the project across the finish line. Initially, when I'd ask him about Bertha, he'd say that he didn't want to deal with her until he was able to do the restoration the way he wanted. I'd say, "Or, we could just get her running again." Two ways of looking at things. Viva la difference.

Figure 14: Totally not kidding about buying my first 2002 in 15 years before the sheetrock was on the walls of the new garage.

But as decades passed, the car became almost an open wound for Alex. It was no longer just a car; it had turned into a poster child for his tendency to accumulate projects and not finish them. It eventually reached the point that, when I'd ask him about Bertha, he'd wince.

Now, this was an unusual situation. People often pine for their old cars. Some even search for them. I, on the other hand, knew *exactly* where Bertha been sitting since 1991—just five miles from my house, in my friend's neighbor's garage (it was like a barn find where I was the only one who knew where the barn was)—but truthfully, I can't really say that I was lying awake at night pining for her. Since getting back into 02s in 2005, I'd become a pretty die-hard round tail light tii guy, having resurrected several from long slumbers and sorted them out. Bertha, the car that started off as a big-bumpered daily driver and transmogrified into a fire-breathing but still big-bumpered molar-loosening track rat, held little special appeal to me. When I'd ask Alex about her, it was more a matter of curiosity combined with a sense of paternal responsibility. However, I'll admit that, in addition to perennial possibility-sniffing that a serial BMW owner like myself lives and breathes, there was also the lure and mystery of reconnection, though I had no idea whether there would be a spark or I'd wonder what I ever saw in her.

Because of my public presence, I'm electronic friends with any number of folks I've never physically met. One such person is Michael Roach. In 2010, when I wrote a column in which I considered buying a particularly challenged car ("The Techno-Violet M3"), Mike sent me the following e-mail expressing grave concern about what this purchase might mean for my readers:

"I was getting ready to board a plane, send out an email to everyone I know in Boston, call the state mental hospital, basically do anything to keep you from getting this car. But fate intervened. Someone up there likes you. This is the car that would have been your undoing. It would have crushed your spirit. It's tragic to see a car guy tormented to the point of hobby desertion. You would have shuffled around staring at the floor for years. The return of Bertha's tender love would have been our only hope, and lord knows where she is. Your family, CCA friends, band, etc, would have still loved you, but missed the old Rob."

When I read it, I laughed out loud, but I told Maire Anne that I'm not sure how comfortable I am with the fact that people I've never met know me well enough to use words like "The return of Bertha's tender love would've been our only hope." However, on the "lord knows where she is" part, as I said above, Mike was wrong. I knew *exactly* where Bertha was. She was still sitting a scant five miles from my house in Alex's neighbor's garage.

I didn't buy that Techno-Violet M3, but ironically, a few years later, I bought something far stupider. In 2013, as a present to myself on the publication of my first book, *Memoirs of a Hack Mechanic*, I picked up a 35-year-dormant 1974 Lotus Europa Twin-Cam Special with a seized engine. I rolled it into my garage, tore out the drivetrain, and began what turned into a six-year-long task rebuilding the engine. The Lotus probably deserves its own book, but long story short, Lotus-Ford Twin-Cam engines are rare and expensive. You just don't find $300 unseized ones or $800 just-pulled-from-a-running-parts-car ones like you would 2002 engines, and rebuilding them so they don't leak is a time-consuming process. I can't tell you how many times I've quoted Michael Roach above and referred to the Lotus as the car that will be my undoing and drives me to the point of hobby desertion. Maire Anne and I began joking that maybe Mike was right, and that only the return of Bertha's tender love could save me from British Mistake #2.

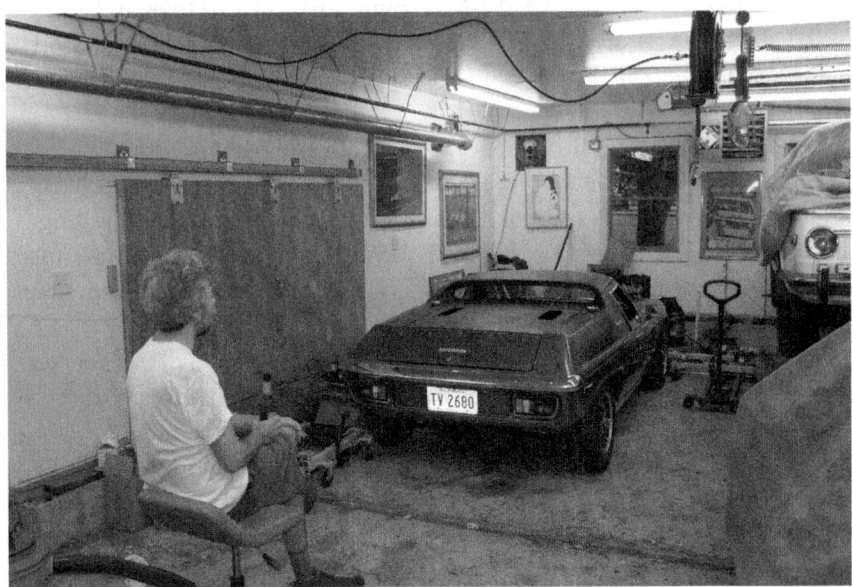

Figure 15: My '74 Lotus Europa Twin-Cam Special, the car that proves that men, in fact, CAN'T be taught.

In the spring of 2018, a number of factors made me turn my gaze toward Bertha. One was certainly the Lotus. Its relative unfamiliarity was testing my stamina to the breaking point. I kept thinking "If this was a 2002, I'd've had it back together and running five years ago." Indeed, in 2017, I bought "Louie," the decade-dead Agave (green) '72 2002tii that was the subject of my book *Ran When Parked*, and resurrected the car where it sat in Louisville and road-tripped it a thousand miles home in the time it was taking me to test-fit the Lotus' front timing cover. I began to long for another project that was familiar—where, like Louie, I could experience the payoff in weeks or months, not years.

Another factor was that, while I was driving to The Vintage in Asheville, I got a phone call from CCA member Daniel Sherron, asking for advice about the steps in starting a long-dormant car. That evening I spoke at length with Daniel, and it turned out he was buying back a highly-modified 2002 he'd sold to a friend in 1992. As we spoke, the similarities with Bertha were astonishing—the sale date, the length of time the car had been sitting, the Webers, cam, 5-speed, on and on. The car was reportedly still an unfinished project, but Daniel said it was in great shape. "I feel like a genius," Daniel said. "It's like I got 26 years of clean storage for free."

A third dynamic was that, the previous fall, I'd gotten a free black '85 635CSi 5-speed (a.k.a. "Black Shark") from my son's girlfriend's father. It sat over the winter, but in the spring, I got it running without too much difficulty and sold it for $3500, so I had windfall money burning a hole in my pocket. Any car guy knows that that money is going into another car before it gets burned up in something stupid like paying bills or replacing living room windows. I first tried indulging my interest in buying an 850i. I really wanted one of the rare six-speed cars, but it's difficult to find these for short money unless they're total basket cases. I found a running 850i automatic in Reston VA for $3500, but I only pull the trigger on sight-unseen purchases in very rare instances, and this wasn't one of them.

Yet another issue was that, while I love tiis, their mechanical fuel injection is all about wind-up. The tii experience is how the car feels and sounds as you put your foot into it, the Kugelfischer injection smoothly does its thing, and the revs climb toward redline. On the other hand, carbureted cars, especially ones with sidedrafts and a hot cam, are all about throttle response, how the car feels and sounds when you mash the throttle and all four butterflies open up and thrust you and the car forward. It's a less refined, more brutal visceral sensory experience. The only car I currently owned with dual sidedrafts was the long-dead Lotus, and it was not going to be running anytime soon.

I looked at a couple of needy local 2002s on Craigslist. Both had rotted frame rails. One was a long-dead tii tribute car (that, long story, I eventually wound up getting for free). The other ran but had so many issues that I couldn't see the upside of it as a flipper. I began to think that if I saw Bertha advertised on Craigslist, with her list of modifications, even dead and in rough shape, I'd drop everything and go look.

These things swirled and combusted in my mind, and on the night of May 28th, 2018, out of the blue, after knocking back a few libations, I sent a very rash, simple, and direct text to Alex. It said: "Sell me Bertha back for three grand. Do it. *Do it.* DO IT!"

Fifteen minutes later, I looked on Facebook and saw that Alex had posted a bourbon-soaked about-to-turn-50 confessional, bemoaning, among other things, how he was surrounded by his unfinished projects. The timing was almost certainly an utter coincidence, but I felt terrible. I immediately texted him back, apologizing for the timing, and promising that I wasn't trying to take advantage of him in a weak moment.

A day later, Alex responded to the offer. The text simply said "Hmmmm."

The next day, Alex texted me again, saying "Still hmmmm ing. Give me a call when you have a chance."

Two days after that, we chatted. We talked about life, time, and the balance between pursuing one's passion versus the sense of peace that can come from simplification. "No pressure regarding Bertha," I said. "I'm not trying to push you into anything. It's just an idea."

"No worries," said Alex, "It's fine." As we spoke and he talked through how he felt about his unfinished projects in general and Bertha in particular, I could actually sense the exact point in the conversation at which he turned. Eventually he said "It's time for me to let her go." By the end of the phone call, I'd made a verbal agreement to buy Bertha back.

I hung up the phone and thought, wow.

I broke the news to Maire Anne. Her reaction was most unexpected. Keep in mind that this would make my 12th car, a nosebleed-high level of automobiles. If ever Maire Anne deserved the "best wife ever" moniker, it was at this moment. When I told her I was buying back Bertha, she didn't say "Are you freaking *nuts?*" She didn't say "You have two other 2002s, and are you *ever* going to get that Lotus back together?" She said: "Oh I *loved* that car! So many good memories! I was thinking of contacting Alex and buying it back for you as a 60th birthday present!"

Best. Wife. *Ever.*

Alex warned me, though, that due to a combination of neglect and vandalism, Bertha's condition had deteriorated from rough to basket case. In addition, he said, the car was surrounded by boxes of old used 2002 parts that had also deteriorated and were falling in on the car, so extracting the car from the garage required first dealing with the parts hoard.

Lastly, Alex cautioned that it was going to be challenging getting Bertha out of the garage and up on the street. He explained that the garage where she was sitting was in the back of his neighbor's house, and that house used to share a driveway with its other adjacent neighbor, but in the intervening years, that adjacent neighbor had built a fence, so to get the car onto the driveway and out to the street, a section of the fence needed to come down.

It was my turn to say "Hmmmmn..."

What Did I Just Do?

On June 2nd 2018, I drove to Alex's house in Brighton to check out Bertha, my old car that I'd just made a verbal agreement to buy back for three grand. As I said last chapter, the car wasn't in Alex's garage; it was in the garage behind his next-door-neighbor's house. I had seen the car just once in the intervening years. About a decade ago, with Alex's permission, I'd gone into the garage where the car was stored and borrowed her fuel pump and distributor to have as spares for a road trip. Oddly, I remembered almost nothing about either the garage or the condition the car was in, but I can sometimes be focused on a particular task to the point of having blinders on.

When I rolled up the garage door to reveal Bertha, I was instantly shocked at how badly the car had deteriorated. She'd been stored uncovered, which is detrimental to the long-term condition of the paint on any car, but that alone didn't explain the dinner-plate-sized rust blisters on the hood. You know those sci-fi movies where aliens vomit acid? It looked like one of them had horked on the hood. Figure 13 on page 32 shows a few small rust blisters, but nothing remotely like *this*.

When I examined the rust blisters closely, I found that in the center of most of them was an unmistakable tufted lump of something, sort of like a bite mark in the middle of a big red blister. Bertha was sitting under a little platform that Alex had built inside the garage. On top of the platform, Alex had stored scaffolding and other building materials such as bats of fiberglass building insulation. I noticed that the little tufts in the center of the blisters appeared to be insulation, and eventually deduced that the cause of the blisters on the hood was that, at some point, the bats of insulation had fallen down from the platform and rested on the hood, and over time had acted as a conduit for moisture coming off the pond that was perhaps fifty feet behind the house.

But there was more horror after the hood: The passenger window had been smashed, glass littered the interior, and there was evidence of rodent incursion everywhere (and by "rodent" I mean "rat" from the size of the turds). And, just to add to the zombie apocalypse aura, the car's headlights were missing.

I immediately thought about Daniel Sherron's comment about buying back his own heavily-modified 02 and getting 26 years of clean storage for free. Clearly I had not gotten in on *that* deal.

At this point, I must quote from my own book *Memoirs of a Hack Mechanic:*

"I'm sure every car guy who ever found a cool car in a barn would give his eye teeth to go back in time, find the owner, hand him a car cover, and beat the crap out of him until he agrees to *go out to the barn and put the cover on the damned car.*"

In this case, I *knew* the owner. It was Alex, and he was standing right next to me.

Figure 16: "A little the worse for the wear" didn't begin to describe it.

Figure 17: Powdery residue from the plaster-and-cinder-block garage was everywhere.

Figure 18: The once-mint Recaro interior had been laid low by rodents, mold and mildew, and a shattered passenger-side window.

Figure 19: Yes, those are rat turds sitting on the Webers' air filters.

After I recovered from the initial shock and got my wits about me, I began sizing things up. Even with the car's awful condition, I couldn't stop myself from grinning ear-to-ear when I saw Bertha's driver's side door still in primer. I donned my traditional Tyvek suit and snapped a dust mask over my face, got down first at eye-level with the rocker panels, and then crawled under the car. Despite the horror of the hood and the interior, Bertha's body seemed remarkably solid. There was a yawning cereal-bowl-sized hole in the driver's side floor behind the pedal bucket (a very common rust-through spot on 2002s due to fluid accumulation from a leaky windshield, leaky brake or clutch hydraulics, or all three), but that was about it; there was just a little bubbling here and there but no other rust-through that I could find. And the engine turned freely. I stuck my head inside, expecting to be bowled over by lethal levels of rodent urine, but while it was certainly fragrant inside, the main smell was, instead, musty.

Figure 20: Driver's door still in primer after 34 years? Check!

I picked as much of the broken glass as I could from the shattered passenger window off the driver's seat and sat in it. The ever-echoing Recaro seat still cradled my butt. The Wink mirror was still there. Even in ruin, Bertha felt familiar.

When something like this happens, people will often anthropomorphize the car and say something like "it needed me." It *did* need me, but I can't say that I felt needy human-like vibes emanating from the car. That's not the car's job. That's *our* job. *We're* the ones who are human. *We're* the ones with the responsibilities to feel something. I'm a deeply analytical guy who tries to make good decisions, but I'm certainly swayed by emotions. My left and right brains tussled in consultation, and came up with this:

There's only one car I drove off from my wedding in. It's this one. That's worth something, right?

Well, what would *you* do?

I could've welched on the agreement to buy her back, but I didn't. Bertha was coming home. She may have looked like an escapee from a Mad Max movie, but she was coming home.

In the very last chapter of *Memoirs,* I say how well-cared-for vintage cars are like a reverse of *The Picture of Dorian Gray,* the Oscar Wilde novel where a gentleman has a portrait of himself in his attic that, with every evil deed he commits, becomes more horrible while his physical appearance remains unchanged. In contrast, pampered vintage cars stay forever young while we, their owners, age. It's like we're *their* portraits in the attic. With that in mind, I had an epiphany about Bertha. I was turning sixty years old about a month after the purchase. I thought, once I get her running and begin driving her around, horrifying purists and frightening children, someone may say "Boy, that car looks like hell, but *you* look great!"

It was the one bit of rationality I could apply to a purchase that otherwise made absolutely no sense whatsoever.

Dealing with the Crap

The first thing I needed to deal with was the fact that Bertha was completely surrounded by stuff. Directly in front of the car was big heavy equipment from Alex's contracting business, things like industrial floor sanders. But along the sides and behind Bertha was a large amount of 2002 parts. Alex, like me, had had a series of winter beater (or, as we say in New England, "wintah beatah") 2002s, and would part them out when they were no longer roadworthy. When you say that a car comes with a parts hoard, that sounds like something positive, but anyone who has had to deal with such things knows that that's rarely the case. Most of the parts are usually, well, crap, and dealing with it all usually just becomes a time-consuming task with smaller rewards than you'd think. And, in my case, it wasn't an "I'll get to it someday" task. I couldn't easily open the doors or skooch under the car until the parts were moved.

In addition to the small and medium-sized stuff in boxes, there was big heavy crap like rusty doors and 2002 four-speed transmissions sitting on the floor like D-Day invasion obstacles on Omaha beach. Alex and I pulled out transmission after transmission, eventually excavating six. When we unearthed one whose bell housing was splintered like a popped kernel of corn, he gleefully recalled when his clutch plate blew up, and how he was glad it didn't take his feet along with it.

Figure 21: Alex posing with the six four-speed transmissions, including the one that self-destructed. A spare bellhousing is seen behind him.

Compounding the problem was the fact that all of the boxes were disintegrating. Because the garage backed onto a pond, it attracted a large population of snails, which in turn attracted rats that ate the snails. Extrapolate this over 26 years, and you probably get the picture: The boxes were littered with snail shells and rat turds and soaked in rat urine. Figurative crap peppered with literal crap and literal piss. It was not pretty. So, even if I *wanted* to carry the boxes into my car as-is—which I sure as shit didn't—they couldn't be carried because they'd fall apart as soon as they were lifted. So they needed to be sorted through.

Immediately. By me. In a Tyvek suit and a mask and gloves. And that's only because Level A Hazmat gear and supplied air wasn't within reach.

The problem with a parts hoard like this is that it *all* needs to be gone through. And, really, even though you know in advance that 90% of it is going to be crap, you need to sort through it to find the 10% that isn't. I once bought a load of parts from a closing bodyshop who specialized in vintage BMWs. When I found a set of new old stock 2002 front grilles and a pair of new old stock tail lights and chrome bezels, all in their original wrappers, I knew that, right there, in those easy-to-ship items, I'd double my money, and I was right. But I still have much of that hoard because the other items weren't worth selling; there quickly becomes a point where the time to photograph, advertise, pack, and ship just isn't worth it. And that stuff was in pretty good shape, not like this sautéed-in-snail-and-rat-turd-and-piss assemblage.

As much as I wanted to get on with the business of moving Bertha, the best way to deal with the parts hoard was to inspect everything on the spot. So I triaged all of the parts into take, toss, and recycle piles. I erred on the side of taking. I organized things on the fly into mechanical, electrical, exterior, interior, lighting, and cooling, and re-packed everything into fresh cardboard boxes.

There really weren't any *schwing!* items like mint new old stock grilles. The closest was the gray pentagonal item on Bertha's hood in the photo above. It's the plastic tool tray that screws to the underside of the trunk lid of a Bavaria. This is the same tool tray that fits in an E9 coupe, and my 3.0CSi had been missing its tool tray for almost 30 years. The four-decade-old plastic tends to be very brittle and cracks easily. So, when I saw the tray peeking out from one of the self-destructing boxes, I immediately pulled it out and put it on the nearest horizontal surface before it fell out of a disintegrating box and the plastic shattered.

In the end, there were three fenders with just enough rust that I wouldn't put them on a car, two consoles, two brake boosters, two sets of stamped steel wheels, two heater boxes, a rear subframe, a differential, a one-piece dash with no cracks but one bad gouge, two sets of beat-up door cards, a few bumpers, at least five windshield washer bottles, round and square tail lights, directional lenses, armrests, visors, exterior trim, a steering column with a key in it, fiberboard trunk floor panels, three instrument clusters, four window regulators, three wiper motors, numerous stalks, switches, and relays, chopped-off sections of wiring harnesses, seat belts, a garbage bag of old door and windshield seals, and a good deal more. If you own a 2002 that you maintain on a shoestring budget and value used parts, it sounds a lot better than it was; almost none of it was in good condition. I didn't really have the room for all this stuff, but what was I supposed to do, leave it there? I took all six transmissions, even though I still have two good-when-removed four-speeds under my back porch.

I dragged everything in the "take" pile over to my house in Newton, and put out the word on Facebook to the Nor'East 02'ers group that I was having a "take it for free" yard sale. I got rid of much of the bulkier stuff that way, including all six transmissions and the somebody-will-want-them fenders.

As much as I believed myself when I said "NO SHIPPING!" I'm a sucker for someone who's long on passion and short on money, and a fellow in Central America *really* wanted the one-piece dash with the gouge in it. I sent it to him for the cost of shipping. He was extremely grateful.

The process in Alex's neighbor's garage only took a couple of afternoons, but the overflow into my garage in Newton created an ongoing aftermath. For months, the boxes of parts were train-wrecked behind the Lotus.

But with the crap dealt with, I could reach Bertha, open the doors, and get on with the matter at hand.

Rolling the Stone Away

Having agreed to buy back Bertha, I needed to get her home.

This was a problem.

Ever since she was stolen in 1991 and recovered with suspected engine damage, Bertha had been sitting in Alex's neighbor's garage, a basement-level drive-in whose entrance was in the back of the house. This was possible because the property sloped steeply back toward a pond, exposing the foundation. The neighbor was an absentee landlord for whom Alex, a building contractor, did favors. The garage used to be accessed via a shared driveway that ran between neighbor #1's and neighbor #2's houses. However, in the intervening years, neighbor

#2 had children and put up a chain link fence to prevent them from wandering too close to the pond, and this fence cut off the driveway from neighbor #1. The lawn behind neighbor #1 eventually obliterated any evidence of garage access. So although there was a roll-up door on the rear-facing garage that allowed Bertha to reach the backyard, there was no easy way to get the car from there up to the street.

Now, I've bought plenty of dead cars, and it's usually not that big of a deal to drag their sorry asses home where you can suss them out and calmly and methodically come to regret the wisdom of your purchase. If a car rolls and you want to move it yourself, you rent a U-Haul auto transporter and tow it with a truck you either own, rent, or borrow. Then you need to get the dead car up onto the transporter. If you want to give your forearms a work-out, you can use a come-along (a manually-ratcheted winch). Since I have the upper body strength of a 98-pound weakling, I instead have a Warn PullzAll, a portable 120V-powered electric winch. So, as long as I'm close enough to a house to plug in the PullzAll, I can push the button and drag the car up onto a rented transporter. If the tires are flat, you bring over a portable compressor and inflate them. If they don't hold air, it's usually not a big deal to swap the wheels for ones with tires that do (and, for a 2002, lord knows I have wheels and tires). Worse comes to worst, if the wheels are seized and the car won't roll, you hire a ramp truck, they back it into position in front of or behind the dead car, and use the truck's bigger winch to quickly and efficiently drag the beached beast up onto the flatbed. If the dead car is just one town over from yours and the tow is only a few miles, it's certainly easier and quicker to just call the flatbed and spend the hundred or so bucks for them to grab it and drop it in your driveway, but if the car is at a distance, economics clearly favor renting the U-Haul transporter and winching the car onto it.

Bertha was just a few miles from my house, but that didn't matter, because neither of the two above-described plans were going to work. The problem was that there was no non-destructive way to get an auto transporter or a ramp truck down into Alex's neighbor's backyard. The car was landlocked back there.

Thus, it seemed that, in order to extract Bertha out of neighbor #1's garage, we needed permission from neighbor #2 to roll back a section of the chain link fence. If that was done, we could get a couple of people to push Bertha onto the lawn in the backyard, point her nose in the direction of the gap in the fence, back a truck down neighbor #2's driveway, use a winch to pull the car through the gap, re-position the truck, winch Bertha up the driveway, and finally, tow her home.

Figure 22: It looked like the only way to get Bertha onto the street was to take part of the fence down.

Unfortunately, we were stymied from the get-go. Neighbor #2 no longer lived there; like neighbor #1, he had become an absentee landlord. Alex's e-mails and phone calls to neighbor #2 regarding the fence went unanswered. So the entire extraction plan suddenly seemed in jeopardy. I thought, what had I gotten myself into? I wanted the car, but the idea of taking boltcutters under cover of darkness to someone's chain link fence in this tony neighborhood near Boston College (which is where things seemed to be headed) gave me pause.

And then, it got worse, because when we tried to push Bertha out of the garage as a test, we found that her rear wheels were completely seized up. So, what? Boltcutters and wheel dollies? Across part of a *lawn*? And for what, this rust-etched hunk of tetanus? And, why? Just because my wife and I had driven off from our wedding in it and it had a bunch of cool parts I'd installed nearly 35 years ago? They say "Choose your battles." I was beginning to think this shouldn't be one of them.

It was at this point that Alex, the visionary to whom all things are possible, mused out loud: "If she ran, we could probably just drive her right up the other side of the house. There's no driveway there, but I think there's enough room." I started off thinking "Hmmmmmn," but like the main plot point of the movie *Inception,* this simple idea, once seeded, gradually came to consume me, at least for the next week.

Figure 23: The other side of the house DID look like it had enough room to drive Bertha up. If she could be made to run.

The idea of getting Bertha running in situ initially seemed ludicrous. "I thought," I replied to Alex, "you said that you rolled her into the garage 26 years ago because the engine was damaged after she was stolen and recovered?"

"No," said Alex," I *drove* her into the garage. Hell, I drove her home after the police found her. She ran; she just sounded like a chainsaw."

"So," I joked, "Bertha—can I say it?—ran when parked!" Alex knew that I'd recently published *Ran When Parked*, the book about resurrecting Louie, the decade-dead 2002tii that reportedly *did* run when parked. With Alex and I standing right next to Bertha, which clearly was in deader-than-the-Wicked-Witch-of-the-East condition (she was not only merely dead, she was really most sincerely dead), we shared a good laugh.

One of the things I say in *Ran When Parked*, and the reason that that oft-used phrase is almost as big of a joke as "that'll buff right out," is that the longer a car sits, the less important the whole "ran when parked" thing becomes, and that, instead, the consequences of its sitting—seized engine, stuck brakes, bad hydraulics, rust-contaminated fuel system, on and on—become the dominant factor. I didn't buy Bertha to "do a Louie" (to resurrect her where she sat and then drive her home). I only did that with Louie because for years I'd dreamed about the adventure;

I'd bought him sight-unseen in Louisville, and rather than pay to ship him, I decided to try my hand at resurrecting him. But the logistics of doing that a thousand miles from home were quite challenging. Any mechanical work is far easier in your own house, with your garage, access to all of your tools, your coffee and sandwich-making materials, and, in my case, my lift.

But here, the situation appeared to be that, in order to extract Bertha from her 26-year tomb, I had to, at a minimum, get her capable of rolling. So I needed to dip at least a toe in the waters of resurrection.

The first problem is actually a linguistic one. Later in the story, I use "resurrection" to refer to the more systematic process of sorting out the car. So, here, let's call it something else. How about Car Potential Revival (CPR)? Yeah, that works. See what I did there? That's why we writers write. The power is intoxicating. (Actually, in the next chapter, I instead call it "le petite resurrection" because French is sexy when you don't speak it.)

I loaded up my daily-driver E39 530i with a small floor jack, jack stands, tools, a MAPP gas torch, and a fire extinguisher, and went over to Alex's neighbor's garage to begin dealing with the seized rear wheels. I didn't realize that I was going to be like a frog in water whose temperature would be slowly increased, and that this was just the start of a week of daily trips back and forth to the garage.

When a car won't roll and we blame it on "seized wheels," we almost always mean "seized brakes." That is, it is certainly possible for wheel bearings to be seized, but they're usually not the culprit—the brakes are. Disc brakes are easier to un-seize than drums because the components in disc brakes are exposed. You can usually knock out the pins holding the pads to the calipers, then tap the pads laterally to un-seize them from the rotors. If worse comes to worst, you can undo the calipers from the struts and pry them completely off the rotors. Seized drum brakes, however, are more difficult because the drum itself covers up the shoes that stick to the inside of the drum.

The tried-and-true method for un-seizing drums is to smack the flat exterior surface of the drum with a small sledgehammer to break the bond of corrosion between the shoes and the inside of the circumference of the drum. Other methods, like backing off the adjusters and using heat on the lip between the drum and the hub, are usually only effective if the drum already rotates and what you're trying to do is remove it from the hub. If the shoes won't un-stick and the drum won't rotate, you have a problem. Some folks go as far as using a grinder to cut away the portions of the drum that the shoes are adhering to. The nuclear option is to replace the entire component that the drum is attached to. On a 2002, that's the rear trailing arm, which is actually not that bad to remove, but on, say, a '60s car with a solid rear axle, it can mean dropping and swapping the whole rear end, which is quite a bit of work to go through, particularly when the car is in someone else's garage and you're just trying to get it out.

Figure 24: Smack those drums!

Initially, it didn't go well, as when I undid the lug nuts to pull one of the rear wheels off, one of the studs snapped clean off. But my fortunes quickly turned, and, with a good smacking, both drums gave it up, and the rear wheels rotated freely. Alex brought over a small air compressor, and we inflated the long-flat tires, three of which were 30-year-old Yokahama A008s, and one of which was the car's original Michelin XAS spare (the fourth A008 apparently had suffered a sidewall puncture during Alex's ownership). I was surprised that they actually held air, but they did.

Bertha was now officially a roller. And suddenly, extracting her from her tomb seemed like a battle worth fighting.

Le Petite Resurrection

With no word yet from neighbor #2 about the fence, the *Inception* thing—the idea that Bertha was actually driven into the garage 26 years ago, that the condition of her engine might not be a showstopper to resurrection er I mean CPR, that maybe I *could* get her running and just drive her out and up the left side of the house—began to consume me. As such, I started to look at things that would normally wait until the car was home.

Oiling the Engine

Now that the car could roll, the next question was: How fubar'd *was* the engine? *Could* it be easily made to run?

When you see videos where people jump-start a decrepit car and crank it until it fires up, it's exciting, but that process can be harmful to the engine. In *Ran When Parked*, I go into a lot of detail on how to correctly start and sort out a long-dead car. At a minimum, you want pre-lubricated cylinder walls, clean oil, clean gas, and no rodent detritus getting sucked from a dirty air cleaner into the engine. The degree to which you carefully oil the engine should correspond with how much you care about it. That is, on a valuable car with an irreplaceable engine, you want to oil the cylinders and then gently rotate the engine a little each day. Since I knew it was likely that Bertha's engine was already damaged, I was a little more cavalier; I pulled the plugs, squirted Marvel Mystery Oil into the cylinders, and immediately turned the engine over by hand five or six times to spread the oil and be sure I didn't feel any obstruction. I then dumped fresh oil over the valve train and changed the oil and filter.

Evaluating the Engine's Health

I'd already verified that the engine rotated freely. Since there was now a compressor in the garage, I ran home and got my leak-down tester.

A compression test will tell you if there's low compression in a cylinder, but a leak-down test will tell you *why*. Also, a compression test requires you to spin the engine with the starter motor, whereas a leak-down test only requires you to hand-rotate the engine to put each cylinder at top dead center. Therefore, in evaluating the health of a long-dead engine, in many cases it makes sense to do the leak-down test first.

A leak-down tester is a very simple device with two pressure gauges. You rotate a cylinder to top dead center, thread a hose into the spark plug hole, connect that hose and another hose from the compressor to the leak-down tester, then turn on the compressor and pressurize the cylinder with air. One gauge tells you the input air pressure; the other tells you the pressure in the cylinder. The ratio of the two gauges (well, sort of; it's actually the output minus the input divided by the input) gives you the leak-down value, which tells you how well the cylinder is holding air.

You might have read that a good engine should have leak-down numbers in the single digits. That may be the case for new or tightly-rebuilt engines. My experience is that worn engines often have horrifyingly-large leak-down numbers—like 25%—and may still run fairly well.

But the real value of the leak-down test isn't in the numbers at all—it's that it lets you find out where the leaking air is *going*. Any old engine will have some amount of "blow-by" air leaking past the piston rings and into the crankcase. While conducting the leak-down test, you can plainly hear blow-by if you take a spare section of hose, put one end to your ear, and the other end to the open oil filler cap or dipstick tube. The gauges will tell you if the amount of blow-by air is reasonable, or big enough that you may have a broken ring, or so big that the piston may have a hole blown in it.

The next place air can escape is past the valve seats. If the valves don't seal, you can hear air rushing past them. If it's an exhaust valve that isn't sealing, you'll hear air hiss out the tailpipe. Similarly, a bad intake valve will cause air to pass out through the throttle body. So, in this way, the leak-down test can tell you if low compression is caused by problems in the block (weak rings/pistons/cylinders) or in the head (non-sealing intake or exhaust valves).

I first adjusted Bertha's valves to make sure that no valves were stuck open because they were too tight, then performed the leak-down test. When I tested number one cylinder, air hissed menacingly out the forward barrel of its Weber. Conclusion: #1 cylinder clearly had a leaky intake valve. This was consistent with an intake valve being bent from someone over-revving the engine, which is exactly what Alex said he thought happened 26 years ago.

Figure 25: Conducting a leak-down test on Bertha's motor.

But the other three cylinders appeared good. And three cylinders should be enough to start a 2002 engine.

We were go for attempted engine start.

Compression Test

The next day, with fresh oil in it, lubricated cylinder walls, and adjusted valves, I dropped in a battery, verified that the starter worked, and did a compression test. It correlated with the leak-down test: #1 had very low compression, and the other cylinders were much higher though uneven. And, while the starter was spinning the engine, I heard nothing that made me think "stop this madness right now before you break something."

Figure 26: A compression test corroborated that something was definitely wrong with #1 cylinder.

So, the toe felt good. Wade in up to the knees?

Checking for Spark

I love the process of resurrecting long-dead engines. Few things are as satisfying as taking hundreds of pounds of metal that hasn't spun in years or decades, and being party to its breathing and spitting itself back into existence. It makes me feel like an automotive midwife.

The mantra is that every car needs spark and fuel to start, and on a car like a carbureted 2002, that's pretty easy. I re-installed Bertha's distributor and coil that I'd borrowed years ago, gapping the points to 0.016". I verified the presence of 12V at the coil's "15" terminal when the key was cracked to ignition. I then hooked up a remote starter switch to the starter solenoid to make under-hood testing easier. While wearing a rubber glove, I held the end of the fat wire coming out of the center of the coil about ¼" from ground, spun the engine, and verified the presence of spark going into the center of the distributor cap. The plug wires were in terrible shape, with some of the screw-in connectors having pulled out of the wires. Initially I replaced them with a NOS set of VW wires I've had kicking around for 30 years, but they didn't fit correctly over the plug ends, so I repaired the plug wires and connectors that had been on the car. I took a spare spark plug, connected a plug wire to it, held the plug's electrode against ground, and cranked the engine. Spark? Check.

Checking for Fuel

You really, *really* don't want to just dump gas in the tank of a long-dead car and see what happens, as odds are the gas tank is rusty and the rubber fuel lines are junk. I use an incremental approach of disconnecting the fuel pump, spraying starting fluid into the carb throat, and seeing if the car wants to start. I'd already pulled off Bertha's air cleaners and checked for debris. I tried opening the throttles, but found that the linkage was seized at the pedal bucket (very common on long-dormant 2002s). I disconnected the linkage rod, lubricated the throttle body shafts on the Webers, and verified that they turned freely. I gave a good blast of starting fluid into all four open barrels of the Weber 40DCOEs while pulling the trigger of the remote starter switch. On a well-maintained car, if you do this, the engine will blast into existence and run for a few seconds and then die. Bertha wasn't that easy, but she did burble hopefully and show signs that she wanted to start. It was enough for me to take the next step.

I unscrewed the tops off both Webers to check the float bowls. When you do this on a car that's been sitting for decades, you may find gummy varnished sediment-laden horror, in which case the carbs almost certainly need rebuilding. Fortunately, Bertha's bowls looked fine (one had a little bit of dry sediment in it which I blew out with an air nozzle from the compressor.)

Figure 27: The float bowls in the Weber 40DCOEs looked nice and clean.

I filled up the bowls with fresh high-test gas from a can I'd brought, screwed the tops back on, and squeezed the remote starter switch. The engine spat and coughed, then caught. With some feathering of the throttle, I had the engine idling. I called Alex over, and we both stood over the long-dead engine, amazed.

Bertha had, incredibly, awoken.

It was a *very* good day.

The Great Escape

Over the next few days, I completed the rejuvenation of the fuel system. I removed the level sensor from the gas tank and looked inside with a flashlight. It looked surprisingly clean, but I pulled the tank out anyway, took it home, threw a chain in it, shook it around to dislodge any loose scale, washed it with water, and let it drain overnight. I re-installed the tank, replaced any rubber fuel line that was either soft or rock-hard, and returned the small electric fuel pump that had been removed from the trunk (like the distributor, I'd borrowed it years ago). I dumped five gallons of high-test in the tank, cracked the key to prime the float bowls, and the car jumped to attention when I started it. Initially, it revved horribly, which turned out to be due to a missing synchronization screw that was allowing one carb to open earlier than the other. I replaced the screw, and the engine began revving surprisingly easily considering the compression and leak-down tests showed that #1 intake valve wasn't sealing. (The video can be seen by searching YouTube for "Bertha's engine running.")

I was now in resurrection's waters up to my waist.

As I say in *Ran When Parked,* although it's incredibly exciting when you reach the point where the engine in a long-dead car is running again, reaching that point is often far easier than the subsequent steps required to get the car moving, much less driving, much less driving safely and reliably enough to take out on a street with other cars. I already knew that the accelerator was seized in the pedal bucket, but I got in the car and tried the other pedals and controls necessary for motion. The clutch hydraulics, miraculously, appeared to function; when I depressed the clutch pedal, it was neither seized nor floppy, and it felt like it was separating the pressure plate from the flywheel (any of these things can malfunction in a long-dead car). In contrast, the brake pedal was so hard that I couldn't tell if it did anything. And the gearshift was completely seized up, fortunately in neutral. I could easily move the shifter laterally, but not forward or back, indicating that the seize point was likely in the linkage, not in the transmission.

Figure 28: The often-troublesome accelerator linkage rod that goes through the pedal bucket.

I spent the next two days dealing with the accelerator and gearshift. Both required working under the car, which was disgusting, and inside the car, which was even more disgusting. My initial impression that the car's aura was more musty than rodent-y was rapidly revised when I needed to spend extended periods with my head down near the pedals.

The pedal bucket accelerator linkage repair is a real pain in the ass. It is astonishing how seized it can get, considering that it's just a pencil-thick piece of metal going through two nylon bushings. Initially I thought I worked it free from the underside by yanking the linkage lever that it attaches to back and forth while drowning the nylon bushings in repeated squirts of SiliKroil penetrating oil, but it turned out that all I did was strip the splines off the inside of the hole in the linkage lever, ruining it. I finally managed to beat the damned linkage rod backwards into the bucket through the bushings. Once it was out, I scraped the rust off it, lubricated the bushings, and reassembled it. I temporarily reinstalled the linkage lever on the end, even though the splines were stripped. Any quick action on the accelerator pedal would likely cause the joint between them to slip, but I wasn't going to be doing burn-outs any time soon. I put out the word on Facebook that I was looking for a replacement linkage lever.

For the gearshift, copious quantities of SiliKroil combined with massive amounts of leverage from a pipe over the gearshift lever freed the linkage just enough to get the car in and out of first and reverse gears.

While I was under the car, I checked the driveshaft. The giubo (the rubber flex disc connecting the back of the transmission with the front of the driveshaft) was cracked. The center support bearing looked okay, but felt slightly bind-y. Both would certainly be changed prior to any real driving, but neither appeared to be an impediment to moving the car a short distance.

I also looked at the exhaust. The HeaderCraft headers I'd installed in the 1980s appeared intact, but the PrimaFlow exhaust was a goner; the resonator was partially broken off at the flange to the headers, and Alex had, at some point, wired it up in place with bailing wire. Obviously, a leaking or missing exhaust won't prevent a car from starting or being driven short distances, but it certainly will make it loud.

With the accelerator and gearshift linkages fixed, I started Bertha, put her into gear, let out the clutch, and successfully moved the car five feet forward and back in the garage. Woo-*whoo*! Bertha was, at least technically, mobile. Normally, you'd then try to move a car 20 feet, shifting gears and testing the brakes, but in front of me was the grassy backyard; I didn't want to make tire tracks without good reason.

I was in resurrection's waters up to my chest. Which was a good thing, because Alex still hadn't heard boo from neighbor #2 about taking down a section of the chain link fence on the right side of the house. The incepted idea of driving the car out of its tomb was now so close that I could taste it. Without a driveway to allow the car to dry its new feathers and test its mobility, it was looking like Bertha's first drive would be out of the garage, a left turn across the grassy back yard, and then straight up the hill and onto the street.

At about noon on Sunday June 10th, 2018, one week after I'd started the in-situ revival I'd never planned on, I went back over and seriously sussed out Alex's comment that there was probably enough room to drive the car up the left side. There *did* appear to be ample room, although it meant driving over a little bit of non-grass ground cover. Unfortunately, a little blue Honda was blocking the place where I needed to drive over the sidewalk and onto the street.

Figure 29: I thought I could easily drive Bertha up this. Wouldn't you?

While Alex and I waited for the ill-placed Honda to move, I decided to try driving Bertha up to the sidewalk. I had a moment of concern when I realized that I hadn't tested the brakes (wouldn't want the car to roll backward into the pond, right?). The brake pedal felt nearly seized, but when I stood on the pedal and let out the clutch, it stalled the car. I decided that I'd let this pass for verification of sufficient braking functionality.

With surprisingly little drama, I gently pressed the accelerator, fed fuel to the Webers, let out the clutch, and eased Bertha out of the garage, onto the sunlit lawn in the backyard, and turned her into position to drive up the hill. It was her first drive in 26 years. But when I tried to ascend to the sidewalk, a combination of stumbling at higher rpm likely due to the bad valve, inconsistent clutch slippage likely caused by rust on the flywheel and pressure plate, and my impression that the tires were slipping and ripping up the yard (they weren't) caused me to abandon the attempt about ¾ of the way up. I let her roll back down. The video can be seen by searching YouTube for "Driving Bertha out of the garage and first attempt at hill climb."

Figure 30: The tire tracks can be seen from the failed first attempt.

I thought, not good, not good. The car, which had been comfortably stored in the garage, was now sitting, exposed, on the lawn in the backyard. It wasn't my backyard. It wasn't even Alex's backyard. I was up to my chin, past the point of no return, feeling exposed, and I didn't like it.

In the middle of all this, a tenant came out of the house and began watching intently. Alex, who is relentlessly cheerful and engaging in all circumstances, explained about Bertha's 26-year slumber under the tenant's feet. I explained, with all of the aplomb of a burglar who'd been caught red-handed, about the car's revival, and that I'd get it out of the backyard soon as I could. The tenant seemed genuinely interested in the goings on, and marveled at the fact that this car had been sitting in the garage under the house the entire time he'd lived there and he hadn't known about it. He didn't seem concerned about the fact that the car was sitting in the yard, or that it had made tire tracks on the lawn and up the side of the house; he was a tenant, not the owner. But he *did* say that the work I'd been doing over the week had smelled up the house with gas and exhaust fumes, adding "That really wasn't cool."

All of a sudden I realized how far out on a limb I'd crawled. Going over there with tools to un-seize the brakes seemed the most natural thing in the world to me. Doing a little more each session, checking for spark, hauling over cans of gas, starting, idling, and running the engine… it never occurred to me for a moment that I'd crossed a line because not only wasn't this my garage, or Alex's garage, not only was it attached to a house, it was *under a house that neither of us owned, and that other people lived in*. It was a wonder that I'd gotten away with it. Perhaps I only did because, much of the time, I was doing this during working hours when folks likely weren't there. It made me realize that if I ever try to perform such an extraction again, it should be done quickly and surgically.

A few minutes later, the inconveniently-placed Honda vanished, clearing a path onto the street. It was now or never. I grabbed the pair of low ramps I'd brought, positioned them at the curb to block out the space, and made the second attempt to climb the hill. Between the car's non-existent exhaust and the mechanical noise from the engine, Bertha *did* sound, as Alex said, like a chainsaw.

But with a lot of throttle and enough clutch slippage to take a year's life off the clutch disc, up the hill, over the sidewalk and curb, down the ramps, and onto Kenrick Street Bertha drove, 26 years after she'd been put away. It reminded me of Uma Thurman when she escaped from the grave and emerged in a cloud of dust in *Kill Bill Vol. 2*. It was an amazing and deeply satisfying moment for both me and Alex. We both laughed, scarcely believing that the car was not only seeing the first light of day since 1991, but that it had driven out under its own power. It wasn't quite Steve McQueen jumping the motorcycle over the barbed wire fence in *The Great Escape*, but it was pretty damned good. (The video can be seen by searching YouTube for "Driving Bertha out from behind Alex's house").

Figure 31: Bertha, sitting parked on the street, couldn't for a moment be mistaken for a normal car.

I posted the triumph on Facebook just after it happened. Friends immediately began egging me on to drive the car the five miles home, but that was out of the question. In the first place, as I say in *Ran When Parked*, the sort-out process involves driving a car five feet, then 20, then a hundred, then around the block, then a mile, then five miles, each time returning to the garage to check for oil and coolant leaks, and likely fixing something. Bertha's barely-functioning brakes alone ruled out a drive on public roads. I appreciated the comment from my friend and professional mechanic Lindsey Brown: "I've seen people cause thousands of dollars of damage because they don't want to spend a hundred bucks for a tow." Second, the car was not only flagrantly illegal, it *looked* like it was flagrantly illegal. I debated whether to try to use my AAA or Hagerty benefits (technically, neither will tow an unregistered car) or borrow a truck and rent a U-Haul transporter, but in the end I opted for speed, legality, and safety, and called a local towing service.

As Alex and I sat on his stoop waiting for the tow truck, still amazed that Bertha was sitting there parked at the curb, we had a brief conversation about price. Or, rather, we didn't. Although the purchase of Bertha had been precipitated by the brash text I'd sent him with a cash offer in it ("I'll give you three grand in cash for Bertha. Do it. *Do It! DO IT!!*"), the car was in much worse condition than either of us had thought, and there was an unspoken agreement, the kind you have with a very old friend, that a renegotiation was not only appropriate, but necessary.

I said to Alex "So, you want to talk about price?"

"No," he replied.

I thought a bit. "You want me to send you my traditional crushingly rational multi-page analysis that looks at the condition and value of the car, adjusts for the facts that you've borrowed my PA for the past five years to run house concerts in your backyard and that you never paid me half the money for the E46 wagon I sold you four years ago, and balances in the innumerable favors you've done for me over the years, including recently saving Thanksgiving by coming over and fixing our oven, and then not read the analysis and instead just skip to the end and look for the number?"

"Yeah," he laughed, "That'll work."

We sat for a bit, taking in the vista that included Bertha on a street it last saw 26 years ago, still not quite believing that she was not only out of the garage, but that she'd driven out onto the street herself.

Finally Alex said "You're the fairest person I know. Just tell me what you think the car is worth to you."

"Fuck you," I said.

Old friends. Can't kill them because too many people would know where you'd hide the body.

Figure 32: A hundred bucks well spent.

About 20 minutes later, the tow truck arrived, and for a hundred bucks, the car was flat-bedded the five miles to my house in Newton. After the drama of le petite resurrection and the extraction, the actual delivery was anticlimactic.

But Bertha was home. Ironically, or perhaps poetically, she came back to the house into which she was denied entry 26 years ago due to lack of garage space. Indeed, she was not only in the garage, she immediately occupied the place of honor on my mid-rise lift.

Figure 33: The long-dead Lotus, nearly obscured by the boxes of 2002 parts that had surrounded Bertha, must be saying "What the...! Why does SHE get to cut in line?"

When I got Bertha home, many folks began asking me what my plans were for her. For a guy who had a recent *Roundel* magazine column that included a series of "Hack Mechanic Tips for Sane Living," one of which was "Be mercilessly rational," I'll freely admit that this wasn't a purchase that made a lot of sense, and that there is no universe in which "restoring" the car makes any sense whatsoever. I usually refer to car purchases as crimes of opportunity, but this was one that I initiated and actively pursued, so I must've really wanted it, perhaps at some deep-seated masochistic level. I do love my historical connection with the car, the story, and the challenge. And I love helping cars be whatever it is that they seem to want to be. When I bought Bertha back, I thought that, if I could get the rodent smell out of her, get her running, get the performance and throttle response of the Webers, the 300 degree Iskenderian cam, and the 10:1 pistons back to what they were in the mid-1980s, and have her be the Mad Max-style go-cart-like troublemaker of the fleet, maybe that would be enough.

But the BMW CCA event "Oktoberfest" was right around the corner (it was actually in July; I know; it invites ridicule), and my Facebook friends and followers almost instantly began egging me on. If one more person said "Have it ready for Oktoberfest in Pittsburgh in July! You can *do* it! Go. GO. *GO!*" I swear, I wanted to reach through the internet and smack them. However, I do take my Hack Mechanic entertainment responsibilities seriously, and the whole "Can he have it ready for Oktoberfest?" thing, for better or worse, rapidly began taking on a life of its own.

Part 2

Le Grande Resurrection

The Decapitation

Although performing le petite resurrection in situ in Alex's neighbor's garage and getting Bertha to the point where she could rise, roll her stone away, and drive out of her own tomb was enormously satisfying (and, when presented online in near real time, entertaining), it really wasn't much more than a stunt, a parlor trick, albeit one born of necessity. I had bet—correctly—that, even with one dead cylinder, I could get the car running and move it under its own power, which solved the problem of how to extract it from a rear-facing garage in a backyard with no driveway access (e.g., rather than construct a complicated cable tow, I drove the car out and up onto the street). But it wasn't as if I was then going to continue to drive it around that way.

So when the car came home to my house in West Newton, after I gave it a cursory exterior washing and interior vacuuming, it was time for le grande resurrection to begin. Job one was to pull the head. Well, I should say that job one was to get as much information as I could about why the leak-down test reported that #1 intake valve wouldn't seal. I snaked a borescope down the spark plug hole, but I didn't see anything egregious like a broken valve embedded in the piston crown or an errant nut holding the valve open. So it was time to decapitate Bertha. And yes, only in the automotive world would decapitation be a precursor to resurrection. Well, that and certain zombie movies. The really bad ones that don't respect the long-standing tradition that if someone takes your head, you stay down.

To me, a big part of the joy of older cars like the 2002 is their simplicity. On a modern fuel-injected car, the amount of electronics and plumbing you need to remove just to get to the point where the head can be pulled is daunting, but on a 2002, you undo the headpipe from the exhaust manifold, disconnect the throttle linkage and choke controls from the carb(s), pull the wire off the temperature sensor, loosen the hose clamps and pop off the hoses, yank the distributor, take out the timing chain tensioner, undo the upper timing cover and pop off the cam gear, and you're basically ready to remove the ten head bolts and lift the head off.

Figure 34: Readying Bertha for decapitation.

Unfortunately, Bertha suffered a casualty in this process. Part of the appeal of the car to me, in addition to the fact that Maire Anne and I drove off in it from our wedding, is the long list of 1980s modifications and parts from *Roundel* magazine advertisers I showered on it back in the day. One of those parts was a set of HeaderCraft exhaust headers which replaced the stock exhaust manifold and headpipe. An exhaust manifold can easily be unbolted from the headpipe and left attached to the head when the head is pulled, but because headers are long, they are generally removed before yanking a head. I could see that the center resonator to which the headers were bolted was rotted clean through, but the headers themselves looked solid. However, when I began undoing one of the three seized bolts holding the headers to the resonator, instead of the bolt turning, the flange turned and twisted right off the end of the headers, badly damaging them.

Once I'd removed the headers, I took both pieces to a local exhaust shop to ask about having them repaired. The shop owner said "I could, but I wouldn't recommend it. The metal in that entire rear section is very weak." He advised that, if I really wanted to attempt repair, I needed to install both the headers and the exhaust to which they needed to mate so the angles could be properly matched. For the short term, I sadly resigned to use a conventional exhaust manifold and headpipe instead.

While I shed a tear for my vintage HeaderCraft headers, I often find it helpful, in resurrecting cars with a seemingly endless list of needs, to envision a time when something like resurrecting the original and highly nonessential exhaust headers will be the most important thing on the punch list.

Figure 35: The vintage HeaderCraft headers didn't survive.

A 2002 head isn't particularly heavy, but as my decrepit body neared its sixtieth birthday, bending over and dead-lifting a head off a block is the kind of thing that angers up my back, so these days I suspend my Warn PullzAll electric winch from a hook that's screwed into one of the ceiling joists, position it over the engine, and have it do the lifting instead of me. After the winch lifted the head to chest level, I swung the head down onto the fender where I could easily grab it, then laid it on a piece of cardboard on the garage floor. The video can be seen by searching YouTube for "removing Bertha's head." (Don't go down the rabbit hole of viewing the other top hits. You've been warned.)

With the head upside down, I closely inspected the valves, particularly on #1 cylinder, as that was the one with bad leakdown and compression numbers. I did not see anything that looked obviously bent, but the #1 exhaust valve had a lighter appearance than the others, potentially indicating that it had been burning.

Figure 36: Close-up of #1 intake and exhaust valves. The light-colored exhaust valve was troubling.

I then turned my gaze toward the block. I smiled when I saw the domes on the 10:1 Eurospec pistons I'd installed in the motor (originally from a '72 tii) over 30 years ago. But what I *didn't* see was any scoring or marring indicating that a valve had kissed a piston.

Figure 37: The pistons appeared free of any indication of valve contact.

My friend George Thielen saw my Facebook post on the head removal and reminded me that it's possible for valves and their seats to look good to the eye but still not seal, and that an easy way to check is to turn the head upside down and fill the combustion chamber with a light solvent. I put a spark plug back in #1 hole, made certain that the cam was rotated so both valves were closed, turned the head over, angled it so the intake swirl chambers were as level as possible, filled the #1 swirl chamber with acetone, and smiled as I saw the fluid level in the chamber clearly drop as solvent drained out through the supposedly sealed valve seat.

Gotcha.

With that, I disassembled the valve train, knocking the shafts out and removing the rockers and the cam, and brought the head, with the valves, guides, and springs still installed, to the local machine shop who does my work. A few days later, Hal the machinist called, saying he found one bad intake and one bad exhaust valve. Unfortunately, he hadn't marked them before he cleaned them, so he couldn't say which cylinder they were from. (Hal's a practical guy. "People will tell you you need to put them back in the same place," he said, "But it really doesn't matter.")

So, although Alex's long-held "engine was over-rev'd when Bertha was stolen and a valve was bent" theory appeared to not be supported by fact, Bertha's engine *did* have damage that required the head to come off (always reassuring, when you've just, you know, pulled the head off). But other than Alex's memories of how the car ran 26 years ago both before and after the theft, there was no way to know whether the non-sealing valves were a direct result of the theft or whether they were a consequence of the car's having sat. As with so many "ran when parked" issues, after a certain point, the historical forensics don't really matter much; what's important is the condition the car is in *now* and what needs to be done to fix what's broken *now*.

I ordered two new valves and had them shipped to the machine shop. While I was waiting for the head, I clocked through the first layer of an onion-like punch list of repairs.

I need to draw a distinction between what I did with Louie and what I was trying to do with Bertha. In *Ran When Parked*, I describe resurrecting Louie in a dramatic one-week period, a thousand miles from home, while sleeping in borrowed bedrooms, using tools and parts that I'd brought with me, and doing everything to avoid ordering any additional parts unless absolutely necessary because of the several-day delay that that would introduce. Because of the unnaturally compressed time frame of the Louie adventure, I was absolutely merciless about which things needed to function (fuel delivery system, cooling system, brakes) and which didn't (heat, handbrake, exhaust, a windshield that sealed in the rain, etc). In contrast, Bertha was now sitting, conveniently, in my own garage at my house, and I had no fixed schedule for her resurrection. While that meant that the time frame for both the repairs and the parts orders could be much more relaxed than they were with Louie, I dove into Bertha with a ferocity that was anything but leisurely. I tend to be that way when engaging a new project.

As I explain in *Ran When Parked*, even if a long-dead car has no engine problems, any car that sits for a decade or more typically has systemic issues with the fuel delivery system (dead or dying fuel pump, rust in the tank and fuel lines) and the brake and clutch hydraulics (seized or leaking master and slave cylinders and calipers, plugged flexible rubber lines). I'd given Bertha's gas tank a cleaning and replaced the filters and any obviously bad fuel lines before I got her running just well enough for her to flee her 26-year tomb and drive up to the street, but her brakes were just barely functional.

As I said earlier, Bertha has a full tii braking system—struts, calipers, rotors, master cylinder, booster, and wheel cylinders—that I'd pulled from a 2002tii I parted out long ago. For a time, tii rotors and calipers had been very pricey, but at the time of le grande resurrection, rebuilt calipers were available for only about $35 each from Cardone, and the rotors were only about $30 each from RockAuto. New rear drums (I hated that they're pricier than the rotors), wheel cylinders, and shoes were also sourced from RockAuto. I already had a set of braided stainless flexible hoses that I used to replace the ancient, hardened, and almost certainly plugged-up rubber lines. The total cost of these braking components was about $350. Of course, it was also possible that the master cylinder itself had gone bad from sitting for 26 years, but my plan was to get the car running, see how the brakes performed, and change the master only if necessary.

The only drama with doing the brakes was that in my haste, I accidentally stripped one of the 6-mm Allen-head screws holding the rotor to the hub; I hadn't properly cleaned out the bolt hole and tapped the Allen head socket into it to fully seat it before squeezing the trigger on the impact wrench. I took some 0.003" shim material, made a cylindrical shim, put it in the Allen hole to take up slack, tapped the Allen socket in with a hammer, and out came the bolt. This technique will now forever be part of my arsenal.

Unlike the brake hydraulics, Bertha's clutch hydraulics appeared to be functional. However, the fact that Louie's clutch master cylinder seemed to work fine last year but then failed at the start of the drive home, just before the entrance ramp to the highway, flashed like a bright red warning sign, so I made a note to order a new clutch master and slave, and planned to change them after I got the car up and running.

Figure 38: Old caliper and rotor. Ick.

Figure 39: New caliper and rotor. Yum.

Figure 40: Old and new flexible brake lines.

Figure 41: 0.003" shim stock inserted into the stripped hole to seat the Allen bit.

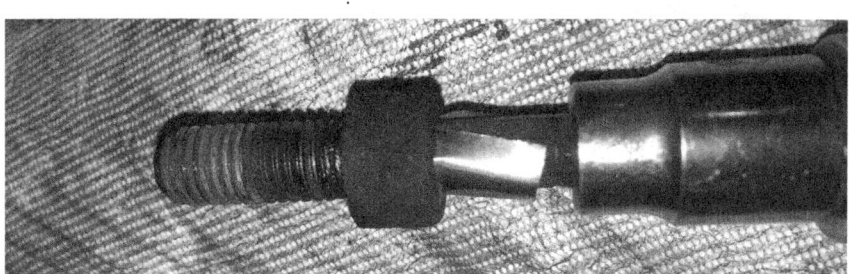

Figure 42: The successfully-extracted stripped Allen bolt.

Figure 43: The frozen shift linkage.

When I was still working in Alex's neighbor's garage, I'd gotten Bertha's seized shift linkage freed up sufficiently to persuade it, with the aid of a pipe over the shift lever, to go between neutral and first, but it clearly needed to be properly unseized. I pulled out the linkage and grinned when I saw that it was a vintage Metric Mechanic setup with bronze shift bushings that I'd installed 30 years ago. Using heat, penetrating oil, and brute force, I got the pieces separated. I then cleaned up the galled surfaces with emery cloth. After re-installing everything, it shifted so smoothly and tightly that I nearly wept.

Figure 44: The shifter and linkage after cleaning.

When I unbolted the front of the driveshaft in order to access the shift linkage, the giubo came out in pieces, which is no surprise on a long-dormant car. With the front of the shaft lowered, I unbolted the intact-looking center support bearing (CSB), gave it a spin, and found it to be very tight. I worked it with Silikroil penetrating oil and it freed up, but I imagined it whining as soon as I got the car up to speed. What the hell, halfway there, right? I unbolted the back of the driveshaft, separated the two halves, and replaced the CSB. The driveshaft, along with a new old stock Goetze giubo I had kicking around, went back in the car.

Figure 45: The giubo was, um, interesting.

Figure 46: Loosening the driveshaft nut to replace the CSB.

I mentioned that I accidentally destroyed Bertha's original HeaderCraft headers while removing them, and that at least for the short term, I planned to replace them with a conventional exhaust manifold and downpipe. A Facebook friend, Kyle Duquette, sent me an exhaust manifold and a few other parts. I almost ordered three new exhaust pieces—headpipe, resonator, and muffler—for an Ansa standard exhaust, as they're relatively inexpensive and I've been pleased with them when

I've used them on other cars, most recently Louie. But I found that in the Siegel Ancestral Parts Heap, I had what appeared to be not only a good headpipe, but, incredibly, a good Ansa muffler for a '75 2002 like Bertha with the center-exiting tailpipe.

There's always risk in replacing only isolated exhaust pieces; the better advice is always "replace it all." But I was trying to resurrect Bertha on a shoestring budget, so I ordered only the new resonator and tried to use the old muffler and headpipe from my parts heap.

However, I found that, as is often the case with used mufflers, the clamp that attaches the muffler to the resonator had squeezed an indented ridge into the inlet pipe of the muffler, preventing it from sliding over the end of the new resonator. I bought a $16 tailpipe stretcher from Harbor Freight to internally press out the ridge caused by the clamp (let's all laugh that there actually is such a thing as a hole stretcher). The results were far from a slam-dunk, but after repeated use of the stretcher, combined with a little grinding with the Dremel tool, I knocked down the internal clamp-created ridge enough that the old muffler slid over the end of the new resonator. I installed the muffler and left the manifold, headpipe, and resonator for when I have the head back.

Figure 47: Yes, there IS such a thing as a hole-stretcher. It's next to the blinker fluid, the muffler bearings, and the metric adjustable wrenches.

Part of the theft damage that had occurred to Bertha 26 years ago included a shattered passenger-side window. If you've ever had broken glass in a car, you know that you find the little square fragments of safety glass *everywhere* for the life of the car. I gave the interior the most thorough vacuuming known to man to get rid of as many of the glass cubes and as much of the remaining topical rodent detritus as I could, then replaced the window.

Figure 48: Glass shards at the bottom of the door.

With the new door glass in, I took the opportunity to clean *all* the windows in the car, inside and out. On a car that's been sitting for decades, clean glass can have a transformative effect. It's like washing off the dust of the tomb. The outside surfaces of Bertha's windows had such a film on them that I literally scraped every inch with a single-edged razor blade before using the Windex. But the effect was stunning. The car went from this:

Figure 49: Decades of grime before cleaning.

To this:

Figure 50: Nothing like clean windows to make a car feel cared for.

A bonus of the thorough vacuuming of the interior was that I found the lenses for the Cibié Oscar driving lights; for some reason, they were hidden away under the seats. Although the lenses were cracked and the bulbs were non-functional, I installed them into the empty headlight buckets that had been adorning Bertha's bumper and looked like errant vertical cereal bowls in search of some cosmic purpose.

Suddenly, the goal of the next hour became facial reconstruction. I installed the spare headlight that Kyle Duquette had sent me along with one that I had kicking around. I rooted around in the boxes of parts and found a set of black plastic grilles. The odds that they were Bertha's original grilles were miniscule, since old photographs showed that the car didn't have the grilles on it even years before I sold it to Alex, but it didn't matter. For the first time in decades, Bertha had a face.

Figure 51: The face of Bertha returns.

At this moment, Maire Anne came into the garage, looked at Bertha's face, and grilled me (pun intended) in a way that was unusual. "What are you doing?" she asked.

"Giving Bertha a face."

"Are those the Cibié Oscars?"

It was an odd question. I do assume that my wife listens to me as I blather on endlessly about which parts I installed today, but I didn't expect her to correctly identify just-installed 30-year-old driving lights. "The ones on the bumpers? Yes, those are the Oscars."

"You need to come inside right now, and come up to the third floor with me," she said. I swear I am not making this up. What, I thought, I've been with this woman for 40 years, and only *now* do I learn that Cibié Oscars are what makes her hot?

We went up to the third floor, and Maire Anne handed me a box. "This," she said, "is from Alan Hunter Johannson." Alan is a BMW CCA member who lives near Winston-Salem whom I'd met only once, quite briefly, but have become quite close with on Facebook.

I opened up the box. In it was a pair of mint vintage Cibié Oscars.

Maire Anne then recounted to me the series of messages that had passed between her and Alan. The lights, I learned, had come from Alan's vintage Volvo. He wanted to send her the lights and have the present come from her, but she insisted that it be his present. He agreed, but recommended that she give me the box when I was having a particularly bad day and things had gone horribly wrong. Her hand had been forced when she saw that I had just installed the old Cibiés.

Figure 52: Me, my wife, and a mint vintage Cibié Oscar, an unsolicited gift from Alan Hunter Johannson.

I immediately sent the above picture to Alan, thanked him profusely, and explained that I'd likely install his generous present when I do the bumper swap, and that at that point, the lights will certainly be the best-looking component on Bertha.

So, quite a lot came together, but I still was waiting to get the head back from the machine shop. And even once I had it, the car still needed all manner of general sorting out. Thus, the odds of driving Bertha to Oktoberfest in Pittsburgh, as people were egging me on to do, were slim (slim to none is probably more accurate). But we do live in a Hack Mechanic universe, where I like to think that all things are as possible as unbidden mint vintage Cibié Oscar driving lights being presented to you, with a hint of salaciousness, by your wife, sent by a CCA member and Facebook friend you met only once.

The Glorious Failure

On the Friday July 6th, 2018, the week before the beginning of BMW CCA Oktoberfest, I stood on the precipice of either achieving jaw-dropping success getting Bertha running well enough to drive to Pittsburgh on Tuesday and ensuring the continuation of my Hack Mechanic legend, or tucking my tail between my legs and saying that it was never an actual goal. Me, I was betting on the latter (I was warming up the slice of humble pie in the microwave).

It was all about Bertha's head. Decapitation is so messy. Don't do it on a whim.

The machine shop's owner, Hal, had told me the head had one bad intake valve and one bad exhaust valve, so I ordered those parts. The exhaust valves in 2002s are all the same size (38mm), but two different-sized intake valves, 46mm and 44mm, were used. All tiis and all post-mid-1972 02s with the E12 head had the larger 46mm intake valves, but early non-tiis with the 121 or 121ti head had the smaller 44mm valves. Since I knew that the engine in Bertha was from a '72 tii with a 121 head (and I knew this because I had rebuilt and installed the motor), I was sure that the head had 46mm intake valves. I was so certain of this that I didn't bother to measure the valves, or ask Hal to.

Except that I was wrong. I ordered the valves, including a 46mm intake valve, and was stunned when Hal called me a few days later and told me that the intake valve I'd ordered was too big. (Actually, what he said was "Whoever you ordered the valves from screwed up." I said, "No, the mistake was all mine.")

"So the correct intake valve size," I asked, "must be 44mm, right?" He measured and confirmed. I immediately got the correct one on order.

I had to think long and hard about the discrepancy. I checked the VIN on Bertha's block, and it did indeed start with 276, verifying that the block came from a tii (an Inka '72 that I'd used as a winter beater in 1984). And, while looking at Bertha's block, I could see where I had blocked off the oil port that originally plumbed the Kugelfischer injection pump. So there was zero doubt that it was a tii block. How could I have been wrong about the head?

Then I remembered that, when I stripped Bertha's head to bring it to the machine shop, I noticed that there was a block-off plate over for the hole for the rod for the mechanical fuel pump. This surprised me, since a tii has an electric fuel pump and thus has a head that doesn't have the hole for that rod. If Bertha's head was from a tii, it shouldn't have needed a block-off plate at all. At the time, I shrugged and thought that perhaps a previous owner of the Inka tii cracked the head at some point and a non-tii head was used.

The more I thought about it, though, the more I realized it was likely that Bertha's head came not from the Inka tii, but from the other major source of her DNA—the rusty 2002ti I'd parted out. This was where Bertha's Weber 40DCOE carbs, struts, big calipers, and brake booster came from. With all the parts that came from the ti, Bertha was sort of a big-bumpered ti tribute car. In fact, decades ago, I took the "2002ti" badge off the parts car and slapped on Bertha. The first two digits fell off some time during Ronald Reagan's second term. To this day, on Bertha's rump, there is a fragment of a badge that says "02ti." I hadn't recalled that that was where the head came from, but it made sense.

Figure 53: Bertha still proudly shows her genetic makeup by wearing her "02ti" badge.

After the correct 44mm intake valve arrived at the machine shop, Hal called me and reported that there was another problem. "You have one bad valve guide," he said. "I'm sorry I didn't catch this when I told you to order valves." It *was* a shame, as it was sure to impart another delay in the project.

But hey, this is the advantage of living less than a hundred miles from BMW parts supplier Bavarian Autosport (who has since, unfortunately, closed its doors). When they have an item in stock, and I place an order in the morning, they usually get it to me the next afternoon. I smiled when I found that they had valve guides in stock. I filled in the address of the machine shop and submitted the order, secure in the knowledge that the guide would be at the machine shop soon.

In truth, even though I was downplaying expectations publicly, I thought that, if I got the head back from the machine shop two weeks before my drop-dead departure day for O'Fest (Tuesday July 10th), it wasn't completely outside the bounds of the possible that I could get the head on, get the ancillary engine components reattached, and drive the 26-year-dead car and sort out enough of its issues to determine whether a 1200 mile round trip to Pittsburgh was smart, practical, possible, unwise, folly, madness, or suicide.

Unfortunately, a few days after ordering the guide, Hal called me and said that the guide that Bavarian had sent wouldn't work without a fair amount of extra machining. He said that Bertha's head had standard-sized old-style valve guides, and that what I'd ordered from Bavarian was a new-style guide in the first oversize. One trivial issue was that the set of valve seals I'd given Hal were for the old-style guides, and that, to use the new-style guide, I'd need to procure a new-style seal. But the larger issue, Hal said, was that he'd need to machine the head to receive the oversized guide, and this might cause concentricity issues with the valve seat, which would add to the cost of the job.

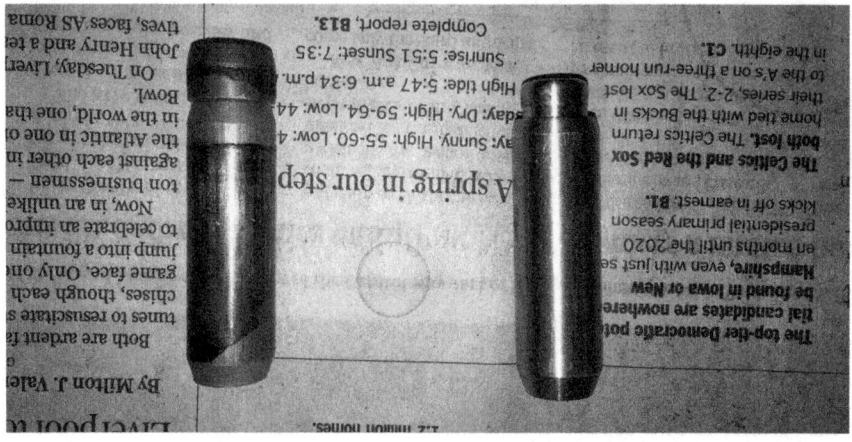

Figure 54: Old-style (left) versus new-style (right) 2002 valve guides.

Now, in the 2002 world, the new-style guides exist because the old-style guides and seals have a reputation for, as the guides and seals wear, allowing oil to get past the valve stems and into the engine when you let off the gas, creating a do-it-yourself James Bond-style smoke screen. The standard advice is that, when you rebuild a 2002 engine, you should change to the new-style guides and seals. That's fine advice, but I was trying to *not* rebuild Bertha's engine; I was trying to get the car back up and running as cost-effectively as possible.

So back online I went. I first posted the issue on Facebook, saying that I needed either a standard-sized old-style guide, or a standard-sized new-style guide and matching seal. Then I searched e-commerce sites for a click-and-buy old-style guide. The only sources I found were an eBay auction in California, and Rockauto. I clicked on the latter.

Rockauto is generally very prompt with shipping, but you don't know where they're shipping an item from until they send you a tracking number. My heart sank when I saw that the guides were shipped via Fedex Ground from California, and that delivery wasn't scheduled until end of day on Friday July 6th.

I called Hal at the machine shop, explained the delivery time and the deadline I was trying to make, and asked what the odds were of getting the head in time to install it over the weekend. "If the guide isn't there at 8am Friday morning, there's very little realistic chance," he said. "And I know Fedex's delivery schedule. It'll likely show up mid-afternoon."

Sometimes, you may not *like* an answer, but with the answer comes clarity. The world cleaves neatly into the possible and the not possible. I found myself far more disappointed than I expected to be that the possibility of driving Bertha to O'Fest was taken away from me (if I failed, I wanted it to be *my* failure), but it meant that I could relax. And besides, I'd just installed a new Walloth Nesch "extra cooling" radiator in Kugel (my Chamonix white '72 2002tii), replaced a leaky a/c condenser, charged it up with good old fashioned R12, driven the car in 93 degree heat, and experienced a cool-running engine and 35 degree vent temperatures. Driving Kugel to O'Fest wouldn't be hardship by any stretch of the imagination. I posted the above on Facebook, preceded by the overly-dramatic heading: "Time of death of the possibility of driving Bertha to O'Fest: 4:45 pm."

And then, something most unexpected happened. On the morning of July 4th, CCA member Jonathan Selig sent me a message saying "Just saw your Facebook note regarding valve guides for Bertha. Let me know if these are the ones you're looking for." He attached a photo clearly showing four old-style guides removed from a box labeled "standard."

Wow.

Except, well, shipping. It was the 4th of July. Even with one-day shipping, if he got them in the mail the next day (Thursday), they'd arrive Friday, still almost certainly too late. But when I clicked on Jonathan's Facebook profile, I was overjoyed to see that he lived in Acton Massachusetts, about 20 miles from my house. I then remembered that I'd been to his house at least a decade ago, looking at the Ceylon 2002tii project car he'd been thinking about selling.

"Could I come over and grab one of these, like, *right now?*" I asked.

In a flash, I was at Jonathan's house. The Ceylon tii was still in the garage ("And thank you for not buying it," he joked). He opened a cabinet stocked with engine parts for whenever he gets around to the tii, and handed me the correct valve guide. I couldn't believe my good fortune.

Figure 55: Jonathan Selig and his granddaughter present me with the valve guide from heaven.

Early the morning of Thursday July 5th, I drove to the machine shop and taped the valve guide to the door with a note for Hal. I then called the shop, expecting to leave a message, but was surprised when Hal answered the phone. He said that, with the guide in hand, if nothing went wrong, he could probably have the head for me Friday morning. And that is exactly what happened. I tried to tip Hal twenty bucks, but he would have none of it. (He did, though, let me give him an air conditioning book.)

Figure 56: Few things are as satisfying as a fresh-from-the-machine-shop head.

I spent all of Friday frantically reassembling the head.

It did *not* go well.

BMW M10, M20, and M30 engines have a rocker-shaft-and-arm valve train configuration in which long rocker shafts go through holes in the head, and the rocker arms, spacers, and springs are threaded onto the shafts. To disassemble the head, as needs to be done prior to a valve job, you need to take a drift such as an aluminum rod, and hit it with a hammer to knock out the shafts. In doing so, you need to be really careful not to bang too hard, because if you mushroom the end of a shaft, you'll have a bear of a time getting it out of the head. It's good to use an aluminum rod as a drift because it is softer than the rocker shaft (better to mushroom the end of the aluminum rod), and to beat on the rod with a rubber mallet, as that softens the blow. But even so, you often wind up slightly spreading the end of the rocker shaft, which in turn galls or gouges the rocker arms' internal bushings as it goes through them.

Figure 57: Knocking in the shafts and threading the rocker arms on them.

If you're using new rockers and shafts, it doesn't matter as much if you mushroom the shafts and gouge the rockers (provided that you can still get the shafts out), but if you're trying to re-use the old ones, as I was, you need to be very careful when you re-fit the components. You're advised to test-fit the rockers on the shafts, and test-fit shafts in the head, smoothing off any mushrooming with a fine file or stone.

Guess what Mister Rushing-To-Meet-A-Non-Existent-Deadline didn't do?

By mid-afternoon, I had the head reassembled, only to find that several of the rocker arms did not move easily on the shafts. I had to disassemble the head and start over. I found that five of the eight rocker arms were badly galled on the inside. Fortunately, I still had the used rocker arms from when I'd rebuilt Kugel's head a few years back. This time I carefully filed the ends of the shafts and test-fit the rockers on them. Finally, by late afternoon, I had what appeared to be an assembled head with a functioning valve train.

Figure 58: I love getting my head together.

The next step was to adjust the valves. It's a little quicker to do this while the head is off, as it's easier to turn the cam. Unfortunately, I found that one of the eccentrics spun all the way around without getting the valve clearance within the 0.006" to 0.008" range. Bertha's head has an Iskenderian reground cam in it, and regrinds typically take material off the back of the cam lobe to make the total valve lift higher; thus making it possible that the adjusting eccentrics might not reach the tip of the valve stem. I'd adjusted Bertha's valves when I'd gotten her running last month, and didn't recall having this happen. It was possible that wear in the pad on one of the rocker arms I'd replaced was just enough to create the problem.

I recalled that 30 years ago, I'd written an article for *Roundel* magazine explaining how, with reground cams or with badly-worn rockers and shafts, you can use Alfa Romeo valve shims (also called lash caps). Sliding one over the top of the valve stem will effectively elongate it and enable the adjusting eccentric to reach it. There are also oversize eccentrics you can buy that solve the problem. I swore that I had a bunch of Alfa lash caps kicking around in my garage or basement, but even after tearing the place apart for nearly an hour, I could not find them.

I seemed to have reached the end of the road of the possible.

Then I looked one more time, and found the lash caps in the very back of a sliding drawer, behind a divider I hadn't previously seen. The lash cap went on, and the errant valve became adjustable.

Figure 59: I found my stash of 35-year-old Alfa lash caps…

Figure 60: …and one of them saved the day. Note the location of the cap at the top of the valve stem.

The next day, I installed the head. And right off the bat, I screwed up.

I set the head on the block, put the oil-distribution tube on, dropped in the ten head bolts, and followed the directions that came with the head gasket to the letter: using the torque wrench for the first phase, letting the head sit for twenty minutes, and then angle-torquing it. A third and final phase would occur after the engine had warmed up.

I then installed the cam gear, the front timing cover, the Webers and intake manifolds, and the exhaust manifold. It was when I was about to lay on the valve-cover gasket that I saw my mistake. Anyone see the problem?

Figure 61: What's wrong with this picture?

If you look at the oil distribution tube, you'll see that I've installed it rotated by 180 degrees; the left side of the tube is sitting in the place where the left side of the valve cover and its gasket are supposed to sit. That bracket is instead supposed to sit beneath the two head bolts all the way to the right, behind the timing gear. D'oh! This is what happens when you rush.

So out came the head bolts, and 180 degrees around went the oil-distribution tube. Head gaskets are supposed to be single-use; if I'd had another one, I might have pulled the head up and replaced it, but I didn't, so I shrugged and re-torqued the head down onto the existing gasket.

When I went to install the exhaust manifold, I found that there was another issue. I was only using a standard exhaust manifold because I'd broken Bertha's original HeaderCraft exhaust headers, and because I live mostly in the tii world, I had forgotten that a stock 2002 exhaust manifold has a threaded port for the almost-always-removed EGR pipe. On this manifold, there was nothing blocking up the port.

I went to a hardware store to find a bolt with that thread size, but they didn't have one. Then I did what I should've done before I left the house: I searched bmw2002faq for the problem. On my phone, I pulled up a post that not only identified the thread size as M16x1.5, but said that the oil-drain plug on late-model Subarus uses that thread size, and even comes with a crush washer. Sometimes you just have to love the connected world in which we live. I asked my phone where the nearest Subaru dealership was, and ten minutes and $6.30 later, a nice gentleman at the parts counter handed me the correctly-threaded oil-drain plug, and smiled as he saw me test-fit it for this unusual application.

Figure 62: The M16x1.5 threads on the oil-drain plug on a late-model Subaru are perfect for plugging up the EGR port on a 2002 exhaust manifold.

By Saturday evening, all ancillary engine compartment components—Webers, exhaust, alternator, hoses, radiator—were installed. I had non-car-related plans for Monday, and was leaving for Oktoberfest on Tuesday morning. That left Sunday to get the car not only running, but driven a sufficient number of miles to unearth and ameliorate any issues.

This also did not go well. In fact, it—the car—basically didn't go at all.

On Sunday, I first changed the sole remaining rubber gas line that I hadn't changed in Alex's garage, the one that runs from the metal gas line at the left frame rail up to the Webers. (Over 30 years ago, I'd installed a high-pressure fuel pump in Bertha, and wanted to use the metal line instead of the plastic one.) I then filled the system with coolant, and fired up Bertha. She started with little effort, but when I checked for leaks, I found coolant dribbling out from what looked like the front left of the head gasket. *Damn*, I thought; *re-using the head gasket was tripping me up after all.*

But then I realized that what I was seeing was probably water dripping out from the coolant neck that's bolted to the head just above that point. I also remembered that the gasket for that coolant neck is shared with the gasket for the #1 intake port, and realized that I hadn't coated the coolant section of that gasket with sealer.

Figure 63: This is the location of the flange where a single gasket is used to seal the coolant neck (upper left) and the #1 intake port (center).

The gasket for this section seals both the #1 intake port and the coolant neck, but for the latter, the gasket needs sealant on it. So off came the coolant neck and the Webers and the intake manifolds. I pulled the gasket off and let it dry in the sun for twenty minutes, then coated both sides of its coolant section with Permatex Aviation Form-A-Gasket. This solved the problem.

I then idled the car to burn the grease off the old exhaust manifold as well as to get the engine hot enough to then let it cool so I could do the final angle-torquing stage, but as I was doing this, I smelled gas. I immediately shut the engine off, and saw a lot of fuel dripping out the front left corner of the engine compartment where I'd replaced the last original rubber fuel line. I re-seated the hose and the clamp and turned the fuel pump back on, and found that the dripping continued unabated.

When I examined things more carefully, I found that the source of the leak was in the metal fuel line itself. Bertha is a heavily patina'd car with a very solid body, but there is one large rust hole in the floor, right alongside and behind the pedal bucket. The leak had occurred where the fuel line ran between the frame rail and the side of the bucket.

Figure 64: This was certainly not good. (The screwdriver shows the location of the leak.)

When a metal fuel line or brake line has rotted and ruptured, it gives you pause. If it doesn't, it bloody well should. What *else* under the car, you wonder, is in this condition?

I sat under the car, and looked, and thought. By this time it was late Sunday afternoon, and I still hadn't driven the car.

Not to be deterred, I used a tubing cutter to trim off the rusted section of fuel line, and ran a longer section of rubber hose to it. (In retrospect, I could've also reverted to using the original plastic fuel line that runs through the interior of the car.) I then re-checked to be certain that this time the fuel system wasn't leaking.

Although I knew that any realistic hope of driving Bertha to Oktoberfest had already passed, I wanted to follow events to their conclusion; I wanted to know if Bertha was going to be like Louie, when, eighteen months ago, on his very first test-drive, the vibe was so clearly, "Yes! I'm BACK! Button me up and drive me to Boston!" Or whether instead the car would feel like a cranky old man awakened too soon from a nap.

I checked a few more things, then lowered Bertha down off the mid-rise lift. I cleared the month-long accumulation of tools and parts that were between her and the garage door, started the car, and eased her forward up to the top of the driveway.

Everything felt wrong.

For starters, the dual Webers hadn't been balanced yet, so there was a fair amount of roughness and engine vibration at idle. And the tires—three Yokohama A008s that dated back to the Iran-Contra hearings and one Michelin XAS that likely knew Gerald Ford—were so bad that I swear I could hear them plotting to kill me during the 50-foot run up my driveway.

Next, the brakes, clutch, and accelerator all felt just on the edge of functionality. The clutch hydraulics—the master and slave cylinders—had not yet been replaced. These are components that, after sitting for 26 years, *will* go bad, as evidenced by my adventure with Louie. Driving on the originals was like painting a big red bulls-eye on them.

In contrast, I *had* replaced all of the braking components except the master cylinder and power-assist booster. The brakes functioned, but the brake pedal travel felt kind of grainy, and I imagined that the granularity I was feeling was the master grinding up and spitting out its atrophied internal seals.

But the worst was the accelerator pedal. Well, no; actually, the pedal itself was missing, since the section of floor with the two metal posts holding the pedal in place had rotted away. Although, while the car was still in Alex's neighbor's garage, I had freed the seized rod that goes through the pedal bucket and installed a stiff spring that pulled the throttles closed, something was still wrong with the accelerator linkage. I would pull up on the linkage to close the throttles and the car would idle at about 1,000 rpm, but after I'd tap the gas, the throttles wouldn't fully close, and linkage would settle with the rpm at around 2,200. Having had accelerators stick open twice, once in my 3.0CSi at Lime Rock at the end of the main straight and once in my 635CSi on a public road, I'm very sensitive to even the possibility of it happening again. More than anything, this was where Bertha's "Don't even *think* about it" vibe was coming from.

I rolled back down the driveway and drove back up to the top. I briefly considered running Bertha slowly around the block, but there was nothing to gain, and only time to lose should she die outside the gravity-fed convenience of the driveway and garage.

So that was it. After several premature reports, the death of the dream of driving Bertha to Oktoberfest occurred for real on Sunday, July 8, at about 7:00 p.m. The following night, I packed Kugel, and on Tuesday, we had a blissfully non-eventful trip down to O'Fest in Pittsburgh.

So, despite my best efforts, it wasn't even close. But in the end, what apparently was important to me was that I had given it my best effort. There was no self-recrimination on being too risk-averse; there was no woulda-shoulda-coulda. Plus, by trying to get Bertha ready for Oktoberfest, even though I failed, I moved things further along, and far more quickly, than I would have if I hadn't given it my best shot.

Bertha's sort-out then continued on a saner and safer time frame. No, it wasn't as exciting as a gonzo road trip would've been, but it's apparently what Bertha wanted me to do.

Barely Drivable

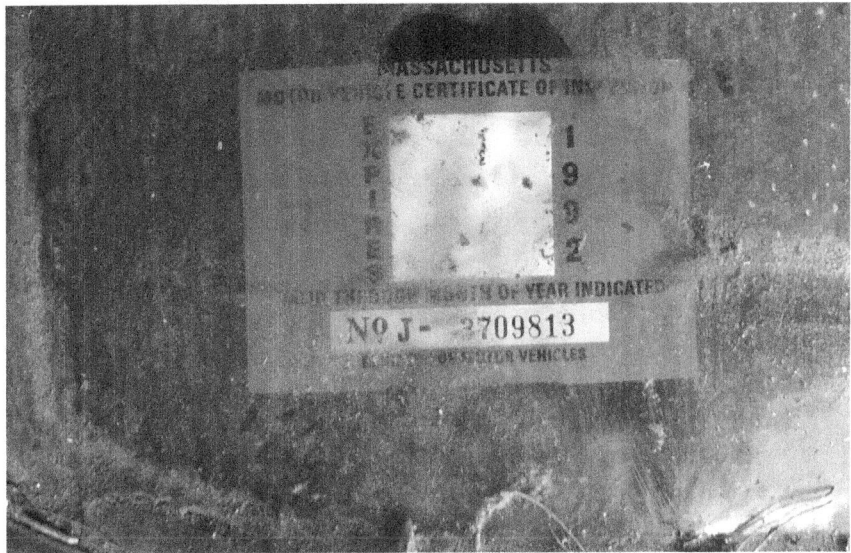

In the last chapter, I described the work I did on Bertha during the feverish weekend just before Oktoberfest. I'd gotten Bertha's head back from the machine shop, assembled and installed it, and, like some automotive Don Quixote, madly attempted to fight my way through a myriad of issues to reach the point where I could drive the car and make some sort of rational decision on whether she was fit to drive to Pittsburgh.

This was, of course, lunacy, and I knew it. No dead-for-26-years car is going to be ready for a 1,200-mile round trip after just a few runs around the block.

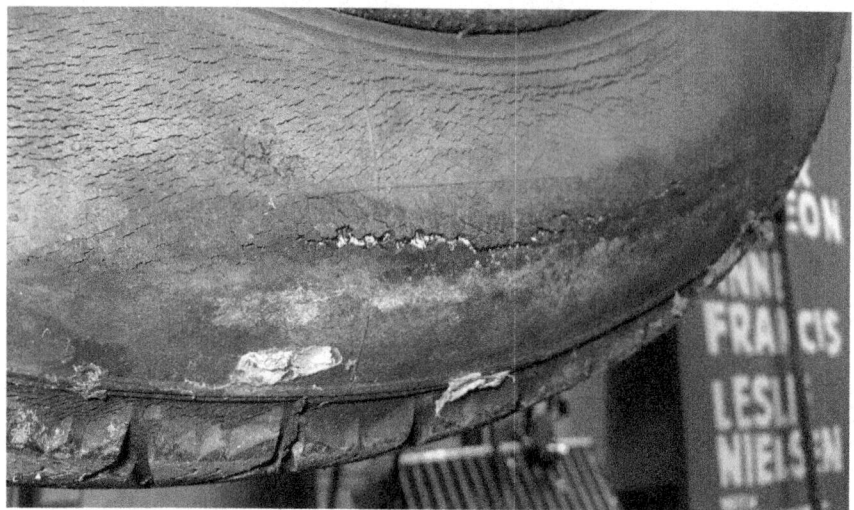

Figure 65: Would YOU drive on these much farther than up the driveway? No? I didn't think so.

So when Kugel and I got back from Oktoberfest, the first thing I did was deal with Bertha's sticky accelerator linkage issue. Fortunately, I found that it was trivial; the sticking was due to the long linkage rod rubbing against the hose between the clutch master and slave cylinders.

Before I fixed it, though, I addressed a related issue from when I'd first gotten the car running in Alex's neighbor's garage. While I was trying to free up the seized rod through the pedal bucket, I had stripped the splines off the lever arm that it attaches to, making it so that the linkage could slip if you mashed the pedal too quickly. A friend had sent me a new lever arm with intact splines, so now I took the opportunity to install it. I then repositioned the clutch slave hose and verified that the linkage moved freely, without binding or slipping. I started the car and revved it, and confirmed that the idle returned to its resting rate of about 1,000 rpm.

With the demons of the accelerator linkage exorcised, I fired up Bertha and ventured gingerly forth from the end of my driveway and out onto the street.

The car was still spewing a visible cloud of oil smoke, as is quite common with engines that have sat for a long time; you need to run them and see if the rings free up and the burning lessens. As I drove the car, the main thing I noticed, aside from the feel of the homicidally ancient and mismatched tires, was a lot of noise from the Getrag 245 five-speed transmission, with a strong whine that accompanied getting on and off the gas and went away when I put the clutch in or coasted in neutral. ("Layshaft bearings," immediately commented my friend Tom Jones.)

I took the car back to the garage, put it up on the mid-rise lift, drained the transmission, and refilled it with fresh Red Line MTL. This in itself was a task, since the 17-mm Allen head fill plug on the side of the five-speed is almost impossible to access with the transmission installed; a standard 17-mm Allen key doesn't clear the transmission tunnel. I took my 17-mm key, cut about 3/4" off the end with a Dremel tool to make a stubby key, slid it into the hole for the fill plug, put a wrench around it, and loosened and removed the plug.

Unfortunately, the Red Line MTL made no difference; the transmission remained noisy and whiny. Oh, well. On the plus side, I thought, it was a good thing that I didn't buy Bertha back as a parts car with a mind to scavenge the five-speed.

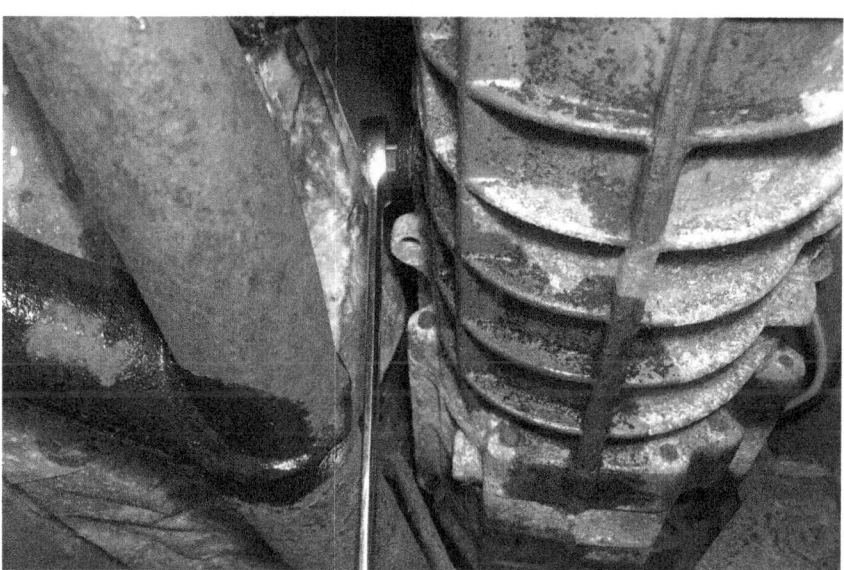

Figure 66: This is how you use a cut-off 17-mm Allen key and a wrench to loosen the fill plug on the Getrag 245 five-speed.

The noisy five-speed notwithstanding, the first drive of maybe a few hundred feet was quite successful. I checked for fuel, coolant, and oil leaks, found none, then went for a slightly longer drive around the block. The tires warned me not to get up above 20 mph, but the car felt pretty good; the carbs were still out of balance, but the engine revved smoothly without obvious stumbling or bucking. The "granular" feeling of the brake pedal vanished with use; the source was probably in the pedal pivot itself and not in the master cylinder. For a longer road trip, the clutch hydraulics *did* need to be prophylactically replaced, but they continued to function.

I thought, damn, if this car had decent tires and a valid registration, I could actually drive it—safely and legally—and see what it *really* needed.

Regarding wheels and tires for Bertha, I had something very specific in mind. There's a look right now that's in vogue—heavily patina'd paint, high-dollar shiny alloys, and low-profile tires that fill up the wheel wells. That's the exact opposite of what I want. My goal was and is to keep Bertha true to her heritage of 1980s period-correct 2002 modifications.

A *Roundel* magazine article 30-ish years ago by Bill Howard on so-called "plus-one" conversions (increasing the wheel size and shortening the tire sidewall to keep the same rolling diameter) mentioned that people had discovered that E30 14" bottlecap wheels bolt right onto 2002s and have the correct offset to fit without rubbing. Nowadays, people laugh at bottlecaps on 2002s, but the later nicer-looking E30 14" basketweave wheels are desirable. However, in the '80s, E30 basketweaves were still too new and too expensive; you didn't really see them on 2002s until the early 1990s.

But back in the day, E30 14×5½ silver *steel* wheels were a moderately-priced addition to an 02; I almost put them on Bertha before I sold her to Alex. Now, unfortunately, they're only available in black. Personally, I positively loathe the look of black wheels on *any* car. I could buy a black set and paint them silver, but they'd look too new. What I want is a worn-in silver set that looks like it's been on the car for 30 years, with the same patina as the rest of the car, as that's what I would've done back when I owned the car. As of this writing, I'm still looking for them.

Figure 67: I want a set of beat-up silver E30 14" steelies like these (photo by Clay Weiland)

Until I find such a set, I took Bob Sawtelle, one of my recent traveling companions to The Vintage in Asheville, up on his offer to extended-loan me his E30 basketweaves with good 195/60-14 rubber on them (these were left over when Bob upgraded to Panasports). I made a quick run down to Marshfield, Massachusetts in the E39, and snagged the 'weaves and tires before Bob changed his mind. While I was there, I met Bob's wife Jean. I mentioned that Bob was kind enough to loan me the wheels he wasn't using. She raised an eyebrow when she heard the word "loan," and playfully advised her husband that the wheels were not coming back to their domicile for long-term residence. I was grateful to be the recipient of the deposit Bob made in the bank account of domestic bliss.

The basketweaves aren't the look I want on Bertha for the long term, but they were exactly what I needed at this stage of the resurrection. Thanks, Bob!

With Bertha wearing rubber that could safely see third gear, all I needed to drive the car in larger orbits was to insure and register it. Running low-speed circles around the block is one thing, but for real driving, these days I have very little interest in exhibiting any behaviors where, if things went sideways figuratively or literally, I could lose my house.

I called Hagerty and added the car to my policy. Hagerty didn't even raise my rates, since the incremental cost of insuring Bertha for three grand, on top of the other eight cars I have insured with Hagerty, didn't move the needle. (I have to laugh whenever I call Hagerty and they refer to "your collection." I don't have a collection—and if I did, Bertha would lower rather than raise its value.)

As I prepared to register Bertha, I discovered a kismet-like ownership issue that accompanied my re-purchase of the car. When I bought back the car from Alex and he searched for the title or a prior registration, he couldn't find either; all he could produce was an old plate-return receipt, but on close examination the VIN on it wasn't Bertha's. After thinking about it, Alex realized that, 30 years ago, he may have played fast and loose with license plates, moving one plate among several 2002s, and may in fact *have never registered Bertha*.

I looked in my old folder with Bertha's paperwork and found my Massachusetts registration for the car from 1985. I slowly realized that, legally, since Alex had never registered and titled Bertha in his name, technically I had never lost possession of her.

In other words, incredibly, not only had Bertha come home, from a legal standpoint, she'd never left.

This was more than just a feel-good issue, because in Massachusetts, when you register a car you just bought, they assess you 6.25% sales tax, and it's not on the basis of what you paid, but on the NADA value of the car. For a long time, the NADA guide didn't accurately represent what vintage BMWs were worth, but then it swung the other way, apparently having in its database the sales of some very pricey cars. The NADA guide reports low, medium and high values. At least Massachusetts assesses you on the basis of the low NADA value, but even for a '75 2002—remember, that's arguably the least desirable year—the NADA low value is the ridiculously high number of $11,300, which would normally result in a sales tax bill of $706. However, if I was still legally Bertha's owner, I didn't have to pay the sales tax at registration time at all, because I'd already paid it when I'd first registered the car 33 years ago.

I took the prior registration and an old plate-return receipt from 1988, both of which were in my name and had Bertha's VIN on them, to the registry. After I stumped two young registry employees with this still-own-it-but-it's-been-off-the-road-for-30-years scenario, a kindly older employee understood, and processed the paperwork in five minutes, assessing me registration and title fees, but not the $706 sales tax. ("We try to be the good guys," he said.) You always get a great feeling when you overcome some challenging title issue and escape from the registry with a fresh license plate for a car, but this one was particularly sweet.

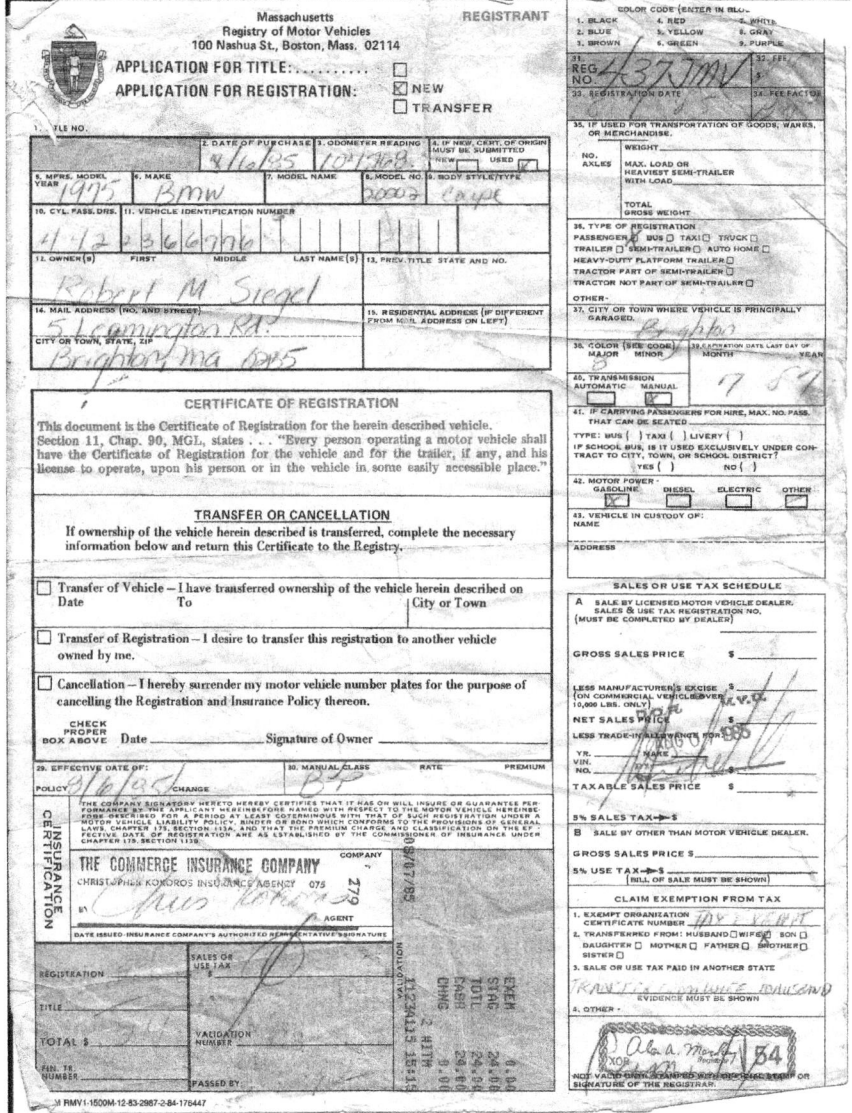

Figure 68: My 1985 registration for Bertha showed that I owned the car and had already paid sales tax on it, and there was nothing in the registry's database that said anything different.

That evening, with a legal plate and non-homicidal tires on the car,

I took several more restrained runs in larger and larger orbits around my house. The transmission was certainly still noisy, but I didn't think there was any danger of imminent failure. And crucially, temperature-wise, with Bertha still wearing her ancient water pump and radiator, she seemed happy, running just under halfway up the temperature gauge even in Boston's 90-degree heat.

After tweaking a few things, I couldn't stand it anymore. My right foot was just itching to mash the go pedal and hear the Webers roar. I threw some tools behind Bertha's driver's seat, made sure that my cell phone was charged, and headed for the highway. I got on the northbound ramp of I-95, and with the car in second gear, punched it.

Holy crap.

When I bought Bertha back, I thought that if the hot engine I'd built for it in the 1980s with the 10:1 Euro pistons, the 121 head, the 300-degree Iskenderian cam, and the dual Weber 40DCOEs was still intact, and if, when I drove it, it still had the snappy throttle response it used to, I'd be happy. With one second-gear plunge of my right foot, I knew: I was happy. The thing just screamed. You can find it by searching YouTube for "first time booting Bertha." And this was with unbalanced Webers and only a cursory attempt at setting ignition timing. It only got better.

On the negative side, there were some substantial metallic clunks over bumps, and I found that the five-speed, in addition to whining, gave a nasty crunch going into fourth unless you babied it. But on the plus side, by the time I got back from the drive, the visible oil burning appeared to be nearly gone. That alone was a major bonus and a huge stroke of luck; I could've easily done all that work to find that, without a bottom end rebuild, the car was a burner.

There were still a thousand things I needed to do to make the car reliable, comfortable, and safe, much less road-trip-ready. In the short term, I needed to get it inspected, which meant that the badly-cracked windshield needed to be replaced.

But in its first fully-legal test drive, it was clear: Bertha was back—ugly, loud, and proud.

(43 Years Old And) Barely Legal

It was ironic that, after the singular unburned hydrocarbon-fueled automotive high of nailing Bertha on an entrance ramp, the next thing to deal with was the mundane but potentially show-stopping issue of inspection. And the clock was ticking, because in Massachusetts you have seven days after registering a car to get it inspected. Getting stopped while driving a car with an expired inspection sticker is, in this state, a moving violation that adds points to your insurance. And the fact that Bertha looked the way she did, complete with an inspection sticker dated 1992 on the windshield, was as good as driving around with a "ticket this man's butt" banner flowing from the antenna.

Motor vehicle inspection in Massachusetts is probably second in stringency only to California. Every car, no matter how old, must undergo the annual $35 inspection. Cars older than 15 years are exempt from emissions testing, but if an old car smokes visibly at idle, they can fail it. As I understand it, they're not explicitly looking for the presence of year-correct emissions equipment (catalytic converter, smog pump, EGR plumbing, etc) the way they do in California, but if an excessively-loud exhaust draws their attention, and if they find, for example, that the car is new enough that it should have a cat but it's not there, they can fail it. Rust is also an issue, as any hole in the body can be cause for failure on safety grounds on the theory that it can potentially allow carbon monoxide into the car.

As I've made clear, Bertha was challenged on several of these fronts.

In addition to all this, Massachusetts augmented its inspection procedure in 2017 to include five cameras in every inspection bay that record the process. If, when reviewed, there's evidence that an inspector passed a car he or she shouldn't have, the shop can lose its inspection license. This caused inspectors to begin do things like jack up the front of the car and check the tie rods, which technically was already part of the inspection procedure but was rarely done by anyone other than a particularly OCD inspector.

Figure 69: The odds of an inspector overlooking the crack that ran the full height of the front windshield were zero.

With all these potential inspection gotchas, Bertha's immediate problem was actually quite straightforward: The windshield was plainly and visibly cracked right down the center from top to bottom. I knew it needed to be replaced for the car to pass inspection, but was hoping to avoid tangling with it so soon because I knew it would be a royal pain in the butt. So, on a fact-finding trip, I stopped in at an inspection station (not my regular one, so I could play dumb), explained that I had a car with a cracked windshield, and wanted to know if I could bring it in for inspection, and get a rejection sticker.

"Yes," the man told me.

"And the rejection sticker gives me 90 days to get it fixed, right?"

"Yes," the man repeated.

This sounded like a perfect way to put off the windshield replacement for a few months. (As my brother-in-law recently said, "Much of getting older is simply buying time.")

Unfortunately, it wasn't true. When I returned with the car, a more experienced inspector told me that you're only given the 90-day period if the reason for rejection is emissions-related. For safety-related issues, the rejection sticker is a different color, there's no grace-period, and you can be stopped and fined at any time by a police officer if they see the sticker on the windshield.

Damn.

So I slid into get-the-windshield-done mode. I needed both a windshield and a gasket, as the gasket in the car was badly cracked and shrunken. 2002 windshield gaskets from Uro Parts are available for as low as $35, but they have a reputation for fitting badly in the corners. OEM gaskets cost three times as much, but their use is strongly advised if you want something that actually fits. With shipping, Bavarian Autosport came in at $128, and the OEM gasket arrived in a few days.

Obtaining the windshield was a remarkable example of reaping the benefits of pay-it-forward. A few years back, a couple, Jeremy and Corinne, borrowed Kugel to drive away from their wedding in (they'd originally hoped to use Jeremy's 2002, but it was still disassembled and awaiting restoration). The wedding was in Narraganset, Rhode Island. A few days beforehand, Jeremy showed up at my house with a race trailer to transport Kugel. The wedding pics they sent me afterward were beautiful.

Figure 70: The pay-it-forward of loaning Kugel to a grateful couple for their wedding got me a windshield

So when I put the "2002 windshield needed" request out on Facebook and Corinne saw it, she forwarded it to Jeremy. He contacted me, saying that he had a windshield from a car he'd parted out years back, and that he could meet me halfway with it. Halfway from Rhode Island sounded fine.

A few days later, Jeremy e-mailed me saying that that evening would work for him, and that he'd be in New Rochelle at about 7pm and could then head north from there. Wait, I thought; New Rochelle, as in Rob and Laura Petrie New Rochelle? I called Jeremy. "I thought we were talking about meeting halfway between Boston and Rhode Island," I said. "What's the deal with New Rochelle?" Jeremy explained that I had it wrong. Their *wedding* was in Rhode Island, but they didn't live there; they were down on Long Island. Jeremy was offering to drive up from Long Island to deliver me a windshield. He was trying to combine it with a visit to his sister's in New Rochelle. Wow.

Once I understood the magnitude of his offer, I quickly looked at the map, saw that Hartford was about halfway for both of us, and began driving there. We did the hand-off of the windshield in the parking lot of a Wendy's off I-95. I said "Gosh, I can't thank you enough for driving all this way just to give me a windshield."

"What are you talking about?" Jeremy said. "It's the least we can do for you having loaned us your 02 for our wedding." In addition to that, the idea that his spare windshield was going into Bertha, which was the car in which Maire Anne and I drove off from *our* wedding, was a remarkable bit of synergy.

With a windshield of such august provenance and gasket in hand, I set about the installation process.

As I said, I expected it to be a pain. I knew this because I did the windshield a year prior in Louie, and it was very challenging repair for three distinct reasons, all of which I expected to come into play with Bertha.

Figure 71: Bertha's windshield gasket was badly cracked, just like Louie's was, but fortunately it wasn't nearly as hard.

First, because Louie had sat outside for many years, its windshield gasket had turned hard as alligator skin, and even after cutting it off with a utility knife (a tendon-threatening operation), the bits of the gasket that remained were so hard that I had to scrape or sand them off. As it happened, I got a pass with this on Bertha. Although her gasket was visibly shrunken and cracked, it cut easily with a knife, and came off relatively cleanly.

Second, once I removed Louie's gasket, there was a little surface rust that had to be wire-brushed off, then neutralized, then the metal primed and painted. On Bertha, the situation was substantially worse. Once I cleaned the rust with a wire wheel on a drill and treated it with naval jelly, several rust holes opened up, ranging from pencil-point size to about half the diameter of an eraser. I posted photos of the rust holes online, proposed patching them with JB Weld SteelStik (epoxy putty), and the responses skewed to the usual cacophony of "Do it once, do it right," "If you don't patch that with a welder, you're an idiot," etc. A few folks, though, were sympathetic, pointing out that that's thin metal to begin with, that with the rust formation it's even thinner, that as soon as you touch a wire-feed welder to the thin metal, you're likely to blow holes in it, and that it's a narrow, curved section, so it's going to be difficult to fabricate and weld in a patch.

Figure 72: A non-trivial rust hole yawned open when I sanded the rust on the A-pillar.

I felt that, with all of Bertha's body issues, it made little sense to concentrate on restoring three square inches around the windshield frame to perfection. I wound up using not SteelStick but POR-15 Patch (seam sealer and filler), a product that has the same rust-binding properties as POR-15 paint. It squeezes out of a tube and smears on like RTV, but dries rock-hard and is sand-able. I patched the holes, leveled out some of the deeper pitted areas, sanded, then primed it using some gray rust-inhibiting primer I have that's very similar to POR-15.

Figure 73: This is the result of using POR-15 Patch to fill in both the holes and the pitted areas, then sanding it level

I chose to not paint over the primer. With the distressed-beyond-recognition condition of Bertha's paint, there didn't seem to be much reason to. After all, Bertha's driver's door had been in primer for 34 years. Plus, at some point prior to my ownership, Bertha had been repainted, and oddly, the color used wasn't the original Polaris silver, but was closer to battleship gray (it's possible they used the darker original color Anthracite). This color disparity was very evident when I removed the windshield gasket. If I ever repaint her (unlikely in the extreme; it would destroy my relationship with the car), I'd take her back to the original Polaris. But, for now, with both Polaris and battleship gray plainly showing around the windshield frame, I just added another shade of gray to the palette. It's just another scar, another part of the story.

Figure 74: A fourth shade of gray goes on Bertha.

You may be aware that, on YouTube, there's a three-part video of our own Mike Self and a few other folks replacing a 2002 windshield at Vintage at the Vineyard in Winston-Salem in 2008. In it, Mike does "the rope trick" in which you put the gasket on the windshield, take a clothesline-diameter length of rope, slide it into the groove in the gasket where the windshield frame needs to go, lubricate the gasket with lanolin-based hand cleaner or other substance that isn't destructive to the rubber, place the windshield and gasket on the car's windshield frame, and from inside the car, pull the rope to "flip the lip" of the gasket so it curls around the inside of the windshield frame. When I replaced the windshield last year on Louie, I found that the car had a DOT-mandated toothed clip on the windshield frame, something that makes the gasket installation more difficult because the lip can catch on the clip instead of cleanly flipping. I've since read that, if your car has this toothed clip, the thing to do is drill out the rivets and remove it. I was relieved when I found that Bertha did not have the toothed clip (apparently early and late 2002s don't have it), but even without it, Bertha's windshield installation was a torturous process.

As I did with Louie's windshield, I sought the assistance of my friend and professional mechanic Lindsey Brown, foreman at The Little

Foreign Car Garage in Waltham, who has installed many windshields and watched glass professionals install many more. There are few things more special in this world than having an experienced knowledgeable friend who is willing to donate a good part of his Sunday to helping you do something you both know is likely to be absolutely miserable.

According to Lindsey, the idea that you just pull the rope and the lip compliantly flips over and you then have an installed windshield is unrealistic. His experience is that most windshield installations are accompanied by some amount of poking and prodding the lip with a variety of tools, followed by pushing and slapping the windshield with an open hand to get it and the gasket to seat in the frame. This was required with both Louie and Bertha. There may be a universe where you simply yank the rope and flip the lip, but I don't live in it. Perhaps the presence of Lindsey, me, a windshield, and a gasket does something to disturb that universe. Whatever the reason, whatever luck I have in this life, it doesn't seem to apply to windshield installations.

Figure 75: Lindsey Brown prepares to help me do "the rope trick."

Lindsey and I had Bertha's windshield completely roped in, but it wasn't quite centered, making the side along the driver's A-pillar a little high, which appeared to prevent the gasket from completely seating.

This commenced the pushing and slapping part of the installation. As Lindsey was shoving the lower left corner of the windshield, I heard a faint *tink,* and saw the windshield—the one hand-delivered from Long Island by Jeremy, the one with the deep human-connected pay-it-forward loaned-a-2002-for-a-wedding-got-a-windshield provenance—crack.

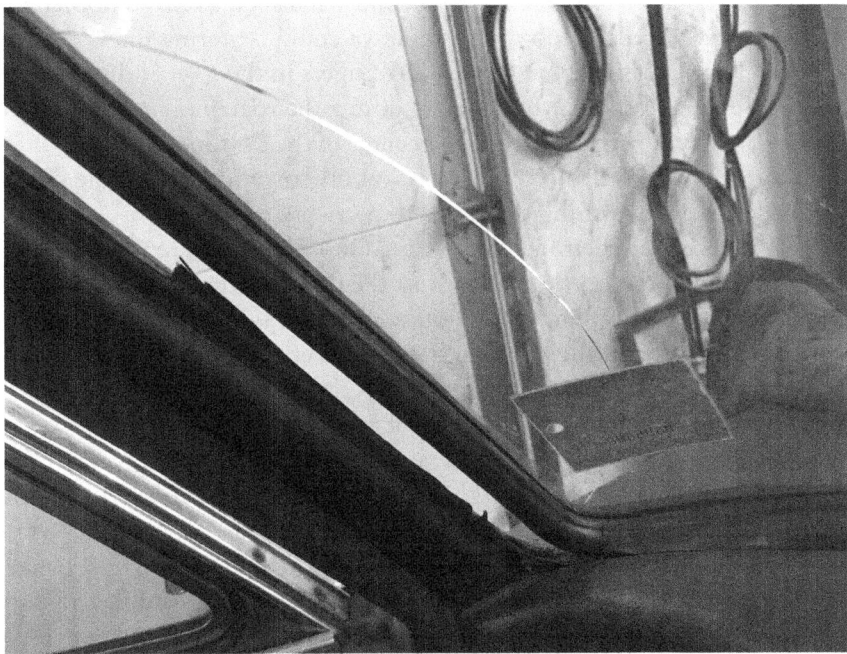

Figure 76: This was definitely not one of those Zen in the garage moments.

We were both hot and tired. Obviously, Lindsey felt terrible. We stopped, said nothing for a bit, and just took it all in. I was wondering whether it might be possible to finish the installation and then bring the car to a glass shop to have someone repair the crack. Then Lindsey suddenly said "I have a least one windshield at work. I'll run and get it and be right back." I tried to protest, but he insisted. I thought that it was an extremely kind gesture intended to try and remedy the unfortunate situation, but, candidly, I did *not* see this Sunday repair session ending with an installed un-cracked windshield.

While Lindsey was gone, I did some online searching. New 2002 windshields are available from the glass company Pilkington. I found one on eBay for $189 plus $129 shipping from Ohio. I was beginning to search to see whether there was a local Pilkington rep from whom I could order the windshield without the shipping charge.

Just then, Lindsey returned, carrying windshield #2. He said it was out of a 2002 he'd owned for a long time and had recently parted out. He laid it on the blanket I had on Bertha's hood. I expected pitted scratched horror, so imagine my surprise when it was a clean, recent-looking Pilkington windshield.

The installation attempt on the second windshield went smoother. We were very careful to do the best job we could centering the windshield, as measured by sticking our fingers in the gaps at the tops of the A-pillars. And this time, we withdrew the rope more carefully, extracting it symmetrically from the center of the bottom and out both directions, and being certain to seat both lower corners of the windshield before running the rope up the A-pillars.

However, once the rope was out and all of the lips were flipped, the windshield was still a little high against the driver's side A-pillar, just like it was on the first attempt. Obviously we were afraid to push on it in the same way that caused the first one to crack. We were stymied.

I said to Lindsey "Well, we have three choices. We could pull the windshield back out and try installing it again."

He threw me a look that could've melted the windshield.

"Or," I said, "I could call a glass installation profession on Monday and have him make a house call." Lindsey nodded.

"OR," I said, "We could install the lock strip and see if that helps the windshield to seat. If you recall, with Louie, we reached a similar point, but once the lock strip was installed, it seated much better." Lindsey raised an eyebrow.

"Did you buy the lock strip installation tool?" he asked.

"Yup."

"Is it the good one with the rollers integrated into it?"

"Yup."

"Have you ever used it?"

"Nope."

"Neither have I. Wanna figure it out together?" We both smiled.

I mentioned to Lindsey that I'd read that it's easiest to install the lock strip if the car has been sitting out in the sun to soften up the rubber gasket. He said something unprintable regarding any assertion that the heat already present in the garage had not already sufficiently softened the gasket.

Search as I might, I could not find a video of someone using the "good" kind of lock strip tool with the rollers, but it was pretty obvious how it worked. With a little lubrication of the groove in the gasket, the lock strip was installed in about 15 minutes.

And with that, Bertha, remarkably, had an inspect-able windshield. I took Lindsey out for barbecue, and strong-armed him into accepting some money, explaining that pay-it-forward is great, but this was *way* above and beyond, and his producing a near-mint windshield on zero notice on a Sunday deserved remuneration. He graciously accepted, saying that what it really meant was that I'd won this round and next time he'd buy lunch. Car friends are the best.

Figure 77: Lindsey hamming it up behind the newly-installed windshield and gasket.

But it made me think about this, my second successful though miserable 2002 windshield installation. Why did I do it again when the first one was awful? Simple: The money. I can't imagine that, had I taken the car into a restoration shop to deal with both the glass and the rust beneath it, I wouldn't have come out at least a thousand dollars lighter. Maybe $1500.

Finally, with an un-cracked windshield, I could try to get Bertha inspected. Before bringing the car in, I did a couple of things that I thought would make her appear more like a real car and less like an escapee from a Mad Max movie. I'd previously removed the a/c evaporator assembly to flush the core and replace the expansion valve. I wasn't quite through rejuvenating it, so the interior looked ripped apart. I temporarily installed a non-a/c center console to complete the interior.

The other issue was the hole in the driver's side floor just behind the pedal bucket. It was shaped roughly like North Carolina, and nearly as large. Since, in Massachusetts, any rust hole in the outer body is grounds for failure due to concern about exhaust gases entering the cabin, if they checked the floor during inspection, I was done for. However, I thought that, perhaps more important than the hole itself was the tell-tale of the missing accelerator pedal. On 2002s, E9s, and other vintage BMWs, the base of the accelerator pedal snaps onto two ball-headed posts that are welded to the floor. It's not unusual for the floor to rot away where the posts are, and thus for there to be nothing for the accelerator pedal to attach to. I did what, even for me, was a particularly ugly hack. I'd already ordered some ball posts that I thought would work (Mcmaster.com, part number 9512K63). I took an old license plate, cut and bent it to approximately cover the rust hole, drilled two holes in it for the ball posts, snapped the pedal on, and sprayed some brown primer on the underside so it might not jump out if a mirror was swiped under the car. Again, the main goal wasn't to cover the hole; it was to provide a mounting for the accelerator pedal.

Figure 78: This was an ugly hack, even for me, but it did hold the accelerator pedal in place.

First thing Monday morning, I took the car down to the local service station where I usually have cars inspected. They know me there, but with Massachusetts' new inspection protocol where inspections are photographed and recorded, they can't do anything for me that would get them into trouble.

I made eye contact with the inspector. He looked at Bertha, and raised an eyebrow that unmistakably said *"That?* You want to try to get *that* inspected?" He walked around the car, made sure it had both license plates and no visible rust holes in the outer body, shrugged, then waved me into the inspection bay.

Figure 79: Even with the front grilles in, Bertha's appearance was certain to give an inspector pause.

It was a nerve-wracking ten minutes. The inspector called me into the bay because the car doesn't have a VIN tag on the inside of the driver's door due to the door having being replaced (shades of when Maire Anne and I came back into the United States from Nova Scotia in our last big road trip in the car in 1987). I had to open up the hood and show him the VIN tag on the right side of the engine bay. I worried that it might be all over if he saw the dual Webers (I imagined him searching for the missing thermal reactors), but he didn't bat an eyelash at them. I held my breath when I saw him jack up the front of the car. But he wasn't looking for rust on the floor; he just wiggled the front wheels to check the tie rods and let the car back down.

And, with that, Bertha received her first new inspection sticker in 26 years.

Figure 80: VICTORY!

Later that day, when the rush hour traffic subsided, I took the car onto the highway and nailed it, as I'd done after first getting her registered a few weeks prior. It felt almost as good as it did the first time.

And, with that, Bertha began a new chapter. There were the Austin years, the endless modifications in Boston, Alex's ownership, the 26-year slumber, resurrection and legality, and now, her bright future.

Her first appearance was at BMW CCA Day at the Larz Anderson Auto Museum in Brookline. Not only did I bring Bertha, we picked up Alex, my friend of nearly 35 years, and *he* drove Bertha there, the first time he'd driven the car since he mothballed her in 1991. He giggled like a kid. Bertha attracted more attention than many of the concours entrants. Numerous attendees had been following the story online, recognized the car, and were thrilled to meet both her and Alex. It was deeply and immensely satisfying.

Figure 81: Alex, Bertha and I had a day we'll always remember at BMW CCA Day at the Larz Anderson Auto Museum.

For the rest of the summer, Bertha and I could be seen and heard tearing up the asphalt many evenings near the intersection of I-90 and I-95 in Newton. The car was hard to miss. Me, I was the guy with the Cheshire cat grin, nailing and wailing on the car that shouldn't even still be here.

In the last chapter of my first book, I say "At the risk of being crass, obviously you can't crack open grandma's chest and stuff a new heart in there. But that's exactly what you can do with a car. You can cheat death. You can spit in its eye. Listen to that baby run. Oh yeah. Suck on *that*, death." Many days, it is a metric shit ton of work and ridiculously expensive doing what I do. There is no balance sheet on earth on which buying back and resurrecting Bertha made any sense whatsoever. But sitting in that faded Recaro, looking out at the ridiculously patina'd hood, and hearing the car scream like she did 30 years ago, it was almost worth it.

Sorting the Charging System

One of my steps in preparing Bertha for drives longer than around the block was dealing with the charging system. This involved replacing the ancient degraded rubber bushings in the alternator with nylon ones so tightening the belt wouldn't cock the alternator toward the radiator, and measuring the voltage the alternator produced to be certain it and the voltage regulator were properly charging the battery. The resting voltage, as measured with a multimeter at the battery (or even with one of those inexpensive cigarette lighter plug-in voltmeters) should be about 12.6V, and the charging voltage with the engine running should be about 1 to 1.5 volts higher, often quoted as 13.5 to 14.2V. If the voltage doesn't increase at all when the engine is running, the alternator isn't charging the battery, and if you keep driving the car that way, the electrical drain from the ignition and other devices *will*

cause the battery to run down and eventually will strand you.

Initially, I wasn't getting any indication of charging at all; Bertha's voltage with the engine running was the same as its resting voltage, 12.6V. Following the steps in my electrical book, I performed the "full field" test on the alternator (jumpering across DF and D+ on the plug to the voltage regulator). I instantly heard the alternator load down the engine and saw the voltage rapidly swing up toward 17V, so the alternator itself appeared to be functioning.

Figure 82: Jumpering across DF and D+ to full-field the alternator (photo from BMW 2002 service manual).

I began looking at the regulator. On a 2002, E3, and E9, the voltage regulator is the old external mechanical style, with contact points that open and close rapidly in order to create an average voltage in the correct range. The regulator is mounted against the fender wall, and is connected to the alternator with a three-pronged plug. That creates nine things to go wrong (three connections at each end, and three wires running between them). Plus, there's the regulator itself, which can stick open and cause the alternator to not charge the battery at all, or stick closed and allow the alternator to run full-field, which will boil the acid in the battery and generate that sickly Sulfur smell. My experience is that, on a car like a 2002 with its original 35 amp alternator and mechanical regulator, you very rarely see charging voltages in the ideal 13.5 to 14.2 volt range, but it should be at least in the high twelves, and when you turn on the headlights and the blower fan and rev the engine to where it would be for highway cruising, it certainly shouldn't drop down below 12.6V. If it does, it's discharging the battery.

I have a pile of regulators, seven of the mechanical ones by last count, and one newer solid-state one. I'm always afraid to throw any of them away, as bad connectors and bad grounds can often make you think you have a bad regulator. (I joke with my kids "Someday, all this will be yours.") Initially, when I tested them in Bertha, *none* of them worked, but once I ran a ground strap from the alternator's case to a convenient bolt on the head, I managed to find two regulators in the bunch that stepped the voltage up above resting voltage. I also found several that were clearly overcharging (voltage readings that zoomed up over 16V), and labeled those as "high." I plugged in one of the good ones, began driving the car, and checked off "charging system" in Bertha's punch list.

Silly me.

Figure 83: Rob's ancestral pile'o'regulators will be my kids' inheritance.

Then, one day, after using Bertha to run an errand, I came out, tried to start the car, and heard that dreaded *click* indicating that the battery had run down. I was only a few miles from my house, so I called Maire Anne. She rescued me and Bertha with a set of jumper cables (Maire Anne and I both joked how it seemed like old times). The fact that the battery had run down meant that Bertha clearly still had a charging issue, and the fact that I had neither jumper cables nor my battery jump pack with me was an indication that I'd gotten kind of cocky about how well sorted Bertha was. I resolved to address both issues.

When I got the car home, I repeated my tests, and still was seeing only weak charging, just a little above the resting voltage. Even though the alternator tested fine in the full-field test, I decided to replace both the alternator and external regulator and buy a more modern internally-regulated alternator. I have these in both my tii and my 3.0CSi, and I've been very happy with them. They remove the vagaries of the external mechanical regulator and its nine additional failure points. They also have the advantage that they put out considerably more amperage than the 2002's original anemic 35 amp alternator. 35 amps may be fine for a bone-stock 02, but add in a beefy auxiliary cooling fan (as Bertha has), high-intensity driving lights, and a modern stereo with a power amp, and you're pushing it.

You can either take your alternator to a local auto electric shop and have it rebuilt with an internal regulator, or buy one that's already been rebuilt that way, or use an internally-regulated alternator from a later model car. At various times, I've done all three.

For a non-tii 2002, you can use an internally-regulated 65 amp alternator meant for an L-Jetronic M30 engine, meaning from a late 70s/early 80s 528i, 633CSi, or 733i. (Note that a tii alternator is different. It's much wider at the pivot point than on a stock 2002, so you either need to have your original alternator rebuilt, or use a 2002 alternator with shims or spacers.) The Bosch part number is AL41X. Rebuilt units are available on eBay as low as $150. Be sure to buy one with a pulley on it, as the pulley isn't the same as the one from the original 2002 alternator. But I saw the equivalent Remy part (13113) for $86 shipped at both Rockauto and CarID, minus a $16 core charge.

The eBay rebuilds appear to have a mixed reputation. My advice is that if you want a high-quality rebuilt alternator, your best bet is to take yours to a local auto electric shop that you trust and have them rebuild it, but be aware that that will probably cost more than an eBay click-and-buy rebuild. (My local auto electric guy has an eBay "wall of shame" showing alternators where the rebuild was little more than a coat of silver spray paint.) However, for Bertha, here, as with many things, I based my decision on cost and bought the Remy rebuilt alternator.

The first issue was that, to my surprise, the Remy alternator didn't quite fit the bracket on the engine. This was curious; I saw no references on bmw2002faq.com to the Bosch unit having this problem. The metal dowel that the pivot bolt goes through was just slightly bigger than the space for it in the bracket. I slightly shaved the end of the dowel with a grinder, taking off less than a millimeter. The alternator then slipped compliantly into the bracket.

Figure 84: The original 2002 alternator (left) and the rebuilt internally-regulated Remy 13113 alternator (right).

The second issue was that the fan hit the portion of the alternator shaft that protrudes through the pulley. This issue *was* referred to on bmw2002faq.com, with some folks reporting that they spaced the fan further out from the water pump using shims, and others saying they ground down the end of the alternator shaft. I looked at it carefully. Bertha has a pretty thick radiator, and the idea of moving the fan closer toward it was a non-starter. Grinding the end of the shaft down was quite a bit more invasive than lightly shaving the dowel through the bushing, but it was what needed to be done. With that, the new alternator fit.

Figure 85: Shaving the threads off the nose of the alternator.

I then performed the minor wiring modification needed to retrofit an internally-regulated alternator, which is to make a short jumper wire with a female spade connector on one end and a male on the other, and connect it from the D+ lug on the back of the alternator to the

D+ spade on the three-pronged plug. This is needed to connect D+ to the alternator warning light on the dash, which provides the excitation current to the alternator.

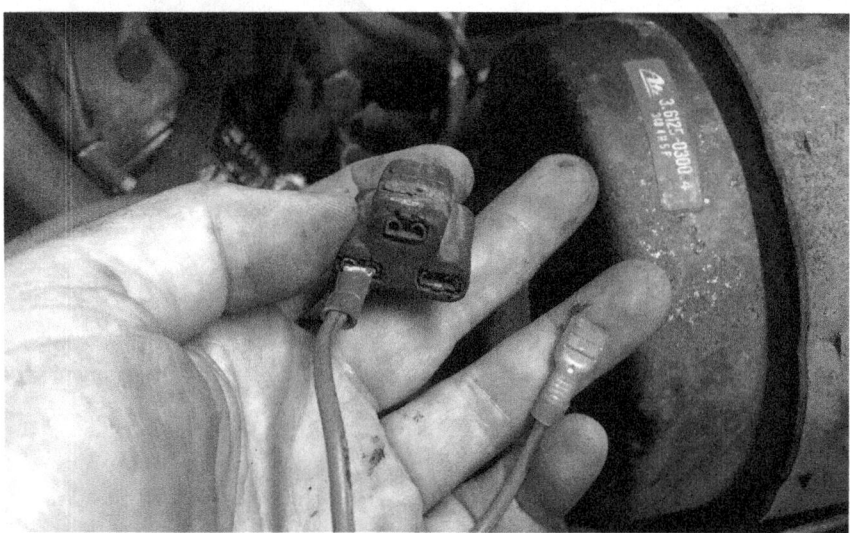

Figure 86: The jumper wire neeed to connect the D+ wire.

Figure 87: The jumper wire in place.

With the new alternator and the jumper wire in place, I started the car, verified that the alternator warning light went out, and checked the voltage. To my surprise, it was low, like just under 13 volts. My experience with newly-rebuilt internally-regulated alternators is that they generally put out the 13.5 to 14.2 volts they're supposed to, instead of the anemic charging of the original alternator and regulator. It didn't seem right. Further, it seemed highly coincidental that the new alternator could be having the same problem as the old one.

I posted the issue on Facebook, and three people (Paul Muskopf, Tom Jones, and Rennie Bryant) recommended that I do a voltage drop test on the positive side (battery positive terminal to alternator B+ post), and if necessary, run a strap from the B+ terminal on the alternator directly to battery positive, as that wire and its connection can become corroded in a 43-year-old car. I did the voltage drop test, alligator-clipping a strap from B+ to battery positive, and found virtually no voltage drop.

Two other people (Rob Koenig and Tony Pascarella) recommended that I do the same thing on the negative side of the battery and alternator. Now, I'd just run a new strap to the head to be certain the alternator was grounded, but I've learned that whenever I think "It *can't* be that," that's a big red flag that a problem might be hiding in a blind spot.

When I clipped a test strap from the alternator case to battery negative, the charging voltage instantly jumped up to 13.6V. The head, apparently, wasn't a good ground. I moved the alligator clip on the test strap from the battery negative terminal, along the negative cable, and down to where it attaches to the starter bracket on the block. The charging voltage stayed at 13.6V. I moved the clip to the head, and the voltage dropped back down. Gotcha. On one hand, it makes sense that the block is a better ground because the battery ground strap runs directly to the block, and the head is insulated from the block by the head gasket, but the head still has lots of metal-on-metal contact with the block. Still, the results were incontrovertible. I moved the alternator's ground strap permanently from the head to the block. Problem solved.

I realized that a bad ground had probably had been the problem with the original alternator and external regulator all along, and that, in retrospect, I probably didn't need to buy a new alternator. But for about $75 after the core return, I now have a new (well, rebuilt) less-troublesome internally-regulated alternator whose 65 amp output is more in keeping with Bertha's new auxiliary cooling fan, and the big Cibié Oscar driving lights, if I ever reconnect them.

So, the fact that I said that I was afraid to throw any of the regulators away because a bad ground often acts like a bad regulator was a bit more prescient than I thought. Maybe, some rainy day when I have nothing to do, I'll put the original alternator back in, ground it correctly to the block, re-test the pile'o'regulators, and throw out the ones that are actually bad. But if I did that, what would I have to leave my children?

Getting Bertha Cold

Surely you don't think I'd go to all this work buying back and resurrecting Bertha, initially purchased in Austin in 1985 partially because it had air conditioning, and not get the a/c working? As Bugs Bunny said to Elmer Fudd, "You don't know me very well, do you?"

I still have the folder of receipts from my roughly six-year ownership of Bertha in the 1980s. One of the little treasures in that folder is this receipt, dated 7/9/1984, from TS Auto Service at 5405 North Lamar Blvd in Austin, for evacuation and recharge. It included three cans of R12 at $3 each, and, with labor, totaled $44.45. Ah, those were the days.

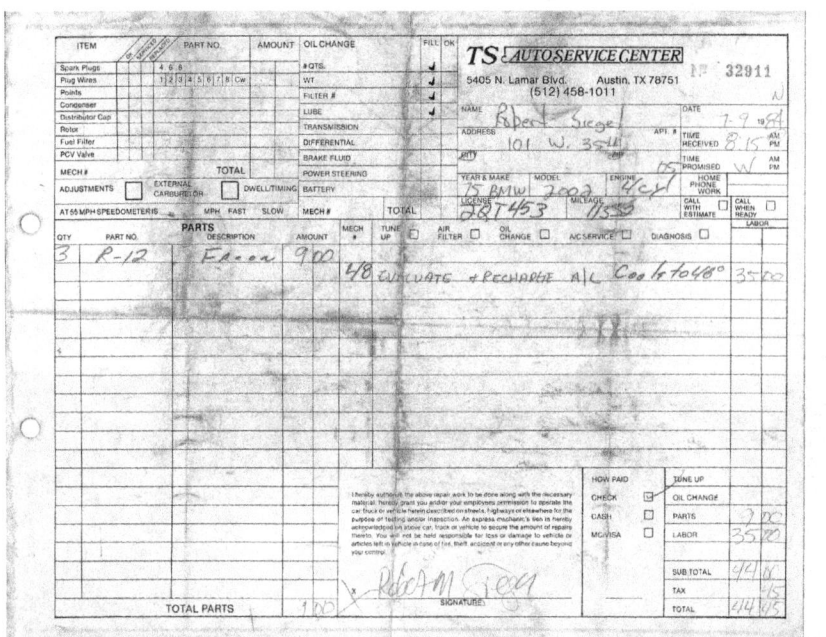

Figure 88: 1984. R12. Three bucks a can. Workshop price to the customer. I kid you not.

I recalled that, after Maire Anne, Bertha, and I moved to Boston, when I installed Bertha's new hot motor, I jettisoned the original York compressor and its miserable bracket that wraps around the front of the water pump, and sprung for a rotary-style Sanden 508 compressor and a correct bracket for it. When I re-purchased Bertha, I found that my memory, or at least that part of it, was accurate; the Sanden and the bracket were still in place.

What I didn't remember was that I, or a combination of I and a previous repair shop, had totally, um, hacked the hose setup. There are four major components in an a/c system (compressor, condenser, receiver/drier, and evaporator). That means there are four hoses connecting them, with fittings at both ends. In examining Bertha, I found that six of those eight fittings were barb fittings, secured by—egad!—hose clamps. In my air conditioning book (*Just Needs a Recharge: The Hack Mechanic Guide to Vintage Air Conditioning*), I write about how, when you change a compressor from an old upright piston model to a newer smaller lighter quieter rotary-style unit, the odds that the hose fittings will match, or will come in at the same angle, are slim, and how you thus almost always need to suck it up and replace the four hoses and not be seduced by the dark side of trying to just cut off the old crimped-on fittings and secure new barbed fittings with hose clamps. So, apparently, back in the day, my will was weak.

Figure 89: Bertha had hose clamps on most of the a/c fittings. Yeesh!

Due to my mistakes ordering correct valves and guides for Bertha's head, I wound up having several weeks of time to burn while the head was in the machine shop. Because it was a particularly hot summer in Boston, I dove into Bertha's a/c rejuvenation with a good deal of energy. In keeping with the low-budget-be-true-to-what-you-did-in-the-1980s-reuse-everything-possible spirit of the entire Bertha project, I decided to reuse the existing Sanden compressor and bracket. As with any a/c rejuvenation, I planned to retrofit a new larger parallel flow condenser and a big cooling fan. For refrigerant, I chose to use R134a because I'd never done a 2002 a/c system with a big modern condenser and R134a, and I wanted to see how well it worked. I'll freely admit that this was an odd set of parameters, but, well, I can be a pretty odd guy sometimes.

But reusing the existing compressor and bracket was somewhere between risky and foolish. The fact that the compressor itself was an authentic Sanden 508 was appealing, since nowadays the market is flooded with Chinese-made clones. On the other hand, those clones sell for as little as $85, and I've never had a problem with one of them. To complicate things, Bertha's Sanden had flare fittings on it, as nearly all of them did in the mid-1980s. As I write in *Just Needs a Recharge*, when you rejuvenate an a/c system and replace major components, you're wise to select parts that have o-ring fittings instead of flares, since o-rings are much less leak-prone. With a compressor, you can re-use the body, remove the "back head" (the thin plate with the fittings on it), and, if it has flare fittings, swap it with one that has o-ring fittings. I've done this previously, but when I tried to do it on Bertha's Sanden, the two gaskets that sit between the head, valve plate, and compressor didn't release their 35-year death grip without shredding, and their remnants were rock-hard. I spent hours carefully scraping and sanding the surfaces clean. I then spent $25 for a new o-ring back head, and another $10 for the gaskets, and in doing so, I didn't have any idea if the compressor itself was still good. Really, with a new Sanden clone being available for $85, it was an absolutely ridiculous choice. But I got it done.

Figure 90: This shows the original flare fitting back head (right) removed from the Sanden 508 (left). The shredded gasket is apparent.

Figure 91: And here's the compressor with its newly-installed back head with o-ring fittings.

The choice of reusing the bracket was even more foolish. The bracket was a copy of the original Clardy Sanden bracket, as was widely available back in the 1980s. Like the Clardy bracket, this one used four pairs of big rubber bushings with metal dowels in the center to isolate the compressor vibration from the engine. Over time, these bushings wear out, causing the compressor and bracket to cock toward the engine. This failure mode was clearly in evidence with Bertha. A fellow by the name of Dave Donahoe, who goes by the handle "hobiedave" on bmw2002faq.com, makes reproductions of the Clardy bracket with the added improvement that the rubber bushings are gone and the bracket instead hard-bolts to the block. If you're installing a Sanden or its clone on a 2002's M10 block, this is the bracket you need. (Note: Steve Peterson from BluntTech now also sells a 2002 compressor bracket.) I even had a spare hobiedave bracket in the basement. But for some reason, I was overly hung up on this issue of keeping true to my 1980's choices and decided to reuse the bracket that was already in Bertha. It was a foolish decision.

Figure 92: This is one of the pesky rubber bushings on the original bracket.

Bertha's rubber bracket bushings were shot, and search as I might, I could not find any source for them. They appear to no longer be made. I measured them accurately and found the closest match in existing bushing catalogs, but no supply house would sell me such a small number of them to try. Then I remembered that when I was at The Vintage in Asheville last May, I'd bought a complete intact Clardy a/c system, and wondered if it came with intact bushings. I opened the box up, and found that the bushings did indeed appear to be in excellent condition. I raided them for Bertha and used them to re-mount the original Sanden 508 and bracket.

I could write reams about selecting a parallel-flow condenser for a 2002, but it's all in the air conditioning book. I decided to use the well-vetted specification that a 10x18" condenser fits in the nose and bolts to the front panel without needing to cut any sheet metal. I used a Spal 30101505 12" medium profile pusher fan in front of the condenser. I often mount these fans directly to the condenser with a zip-tie kit, but the fan seemed a bit heavy for that, so I bolted it to the hood supports instead.

Figure 93: The 10x18" parallel-flow condenser and Spal 12" fan fit in Bertha's nose without needing to cut anything.

That left the evaporator and expansion valve. As I say in the book, if you want to be sure (well, as sure as possible) that an a/c system will blow cold when you assemble and charge it, you should remove the evaporator assembly, disassemble it, flush the evaporator core, and replace the expansion valve. However, if you don't see any evidence of contamination in the a/c hoses (no metal shavings, no oily or powdered residue), and if you're not changing the type of refrigerant oil being used, you can chance it and leave the evaporator intact. The hoses looked uncontaminated, but I *was* planning on switching from R12 and mineral oil to R134a and ester oil. This meant that the evaporator needed to be disassembled and the core flushed.

There were two other reasons to yank the evap assembly. First, with the high degree of rodent contamination in Bertha, I fully expected the evaporator assembly to be full of acorns, snail shells, nests, dung, dead little rodent bodies, etc. I was stunned to find that it was clean as a whistle inside. I theorized that this was an odd benefit of the fact that the rodents in the garage where Alex had stored Bertha were rats, not mice, and were probably too large to get inside the evap assembly.

Second, the evap assembly sits behind the heater box. 2002 heater boxes frequently need to be removed and rebuilt to replace a dead blower motor and to re-line the flaps with rubber foam so they seal and don't let hot outside air in. Bertha's heater box suffered both of these maladies. So, since, on a 2002, yanking the evaporator assembly is easy (as opposed to on an E9 where it's a bloody pain), out it came. I disassembled it, and cleaned and flushed the evaporator core.

Figure 94: It's very satisfying to flush an evaporator core. You know it's clean.

Figure 95: I cleaned and reused the original expansion valve.

For the expansion valve, I try to use original Egelhof valves, stamped "Made in West Germany," but these are getting harder and pricier to come by. I thought I found one, but when it arrived, it had a "Made in China" label on it. Instead of using it, I cleaned the old Egelhof valve, made sure I could blow through it (which only ensures that it's open; it doesn't ensure that it can move), verified that the blower fan worked, reassembled the evaporator assembly, and hoped that I'd made the right choice.

When I got Bertha's head back from the machine shop in July, my a/c work stopped, as the main event—resurrecting Bertha herself, not her a/c system—returned to center stage. But once I'd gotten Bertha over the hump and began driving her around in Boston's biblically-hot summer, I knew that in a few repair sessions I could finish the a/c installation, charge it up, and see if the choices I'd made produced a functioning system or if I had to tear it open again.

Interestingly, what I *didn't* do was remove, rebuild, and reinstall the heater box, even though it made perfect sense to do so while the evap assembly was out, and even though I'd already bought a blower motor for it. I knew that I could get it done in three easy sessions (one to remove, one to rebuild, and one to reinstall), but, fundamentally, I just didn't feel like doing it. Plus, by this time, we were in the middle of an August heat wave in Boston. Who the hell cared about any auto repair related to working *heat?* I rotated the foot-well flaps open, peered in, sniffed, verified that, like the evap assembly, the heater box appeared to be free of rodent detritus, then taped the foot-well openings shut with easy-to-remove packing tape so they wouldn't let hot outside air into the cabin.

I then reinstalled the evaporator assembly, installed a generic o-ring drier where the old one had been, and used my Mastercool Hydra-Krimp 71500 to make the four hoses, all cut to length and crimped in the car. I also found and installed a set of a/c console side pieces that had been missing from Bertha for 30 years. Suddenly, despite the shredded Recaros and the faded carpet, the interior had a completeness to it that it hadn't had since I first purchased the car in Austin in 1984.

Figure 96: With the a/c console side pieces installed, Bertha's interior suddenly looked complete.

One of the things I discuss in the air conditioning book is the advantage of prophylactically pressure-testing an a/c system with nitrogen, how it works better at finding leaks than pulling a vacuum or than using dye. I say that, if you pressurize the system to 120 psi (the maximum reading on the low-pressure gauge) and let it sit overnight, if it drops by one psi, that could just be a change in pressure due to a temperature drop in your garage, but if it drops by five psi, you're in denial if you don't think it has a leak. I pressure-tested Bertha overnight, and it dropped by an amount right in the middle, 2 1/2 psi. I thought "Is this a test?" I sprayed Big Blu soap solution on all of the connections, but did not see any bubbles anywhere. I decided that I could either chase a leak that I wasn't even certain was there, or evacuate and charge it and see if my reused compressor and expansion valve worked. I opted for the latter.

After doing a/c work, it's always a big relief to see the high-pressure gauge go high and the low-pressure gauge go low as you're charging a system up with refrigerant, indicating that the system is working. And that's what I saw. Considering my risky choices of re-using both the compressor and expansion valve, I was elated.

But as I was shooting in the second can of R134a, I heard a loud hissing from the front of the engine compartment. I saw liquid refrigerant shooting out the inlet connection to the drier. What the?! I shut the car off, grabbed a wrench, and tightened the connection. The leak stopped. Apparently, when I installed this hose, I'd mistaken some tightness in the threads for a sealed o-ring fitting and hadn't snugged the thing all the way down. I made double sure that it was snug now, and continued to charge the system. I thought it was likely that this had been the source of my mysterious 2 1/2 psi overnight pressure drop.

That afternoon, I had 42 degree vent temperatures. It wasn't the meat-freezing 32 degrees I was getting in Kugel with its R12 system, but it was damned fine for R134a. Not only was Bertha back, she was cool as a cucumber.

The a/c worked fine until I replaced the alternator, as I described in the previous chapter. Largely coincidentally, when I turned on the a/c to see how the new alternator reacted to the electrical load from the big Spal fan, I heard a noise that sounded like a chainsaw. It turned out to be due to the compressor belt being loose and alternately slipping and grabbing. I tightened the belt, but immediately saw a major problem: With the belt tight, the compressor and bracket were not only cocked out of alignment with the engine, the compressor pulley was hitting the big Suspension Techniques front sway bar. The root cause of this was clearly my odd and unwise choice of reusing the original bracket and mounted to the block with rubber bushings. Even though I thought I had installed a good set of bushings, in just a few weeks they'd caused the bracket to cock.

Figure 97: I HATE rubber bushings on compressor brackets.

So I did what I should've done at the beginning—I installed the bushing-free "hobiedave" bracket that I had sitting in my basement. It's a little bit of a dance replacing the bracket with the hoses still on the compressor (the system was already charged up and functioning), but in one hot and sweaty repair session, I got it done.

Figure 98: The original bushing-laden bracket (right) and Hobiedave bracket (left).

Figure 99: Saved by Hobiedave!

So, Bertha was not only running, she was chill. My hope was to get a road trip out of her before I needed to worry about that heater box I should've rebuilt when I had the chance.

Fear of Flying

There I was, a little over three months after rescuing Bertha from Alex's neighbor's garage in which she sat for 26 years. I rolled the stone away, resurrected her, and drove her out of the cave back in June 2018, but the point at which she was street-drivable was late July. After a few big repairs and a myriad of small ones, the car not only ran, but went like a bat out of hell. With the new internally-regulated alternator and working a/c, things had reached the point where I could simply get in it, twist the key, aim the cold air at my face, drive her, hear those Weber 40DCOEs open up loud and snotty, and smile. And, with the installation of the beveled 47mm dust caps on Bertha's tii front rotors, I even got the center caps to fit on the basketweaves, making her look almost civilized. (Google "Avonride 47mm dust caps" and you'll find sources for them in England.)

Make no mistake, Bertha was still a total rat, but she was a mostly-functional total rat. I still kept a few tools on the floor behind the driver's seat, but I no longer felt it was necessary to, for example, always keep the cigarette lighter voltmeter plugged in to monitor charging voltage, or always have two 13mm wrenches within reach at all times to tighten up what had been a perennially-slipping alternator belt if I was just running out to buy beer.

So, what was left?

Well, obviously, a road trip. An adventure. Maybe a small one for starters.

And what would prevent me from hitting the road with Bertha and having said small adventure?

Well, obviously, addressing the stuff that wasn't easily addressable.

Okay, there *were* still two small prophylactic maintenance issues. Maybe three. I would've been an idiot not to replace the clutch hydraulics that sat for 26 years. The ones on Louie failed just as I began the thousand-mile drive home from Louisville last year. Fool me once and all that. The master and slave together are maybe a hundred bucks. This is a repair best done at home, not parts you throw into the trunk in case they fail on the road. Likewise with the water pump. It seemed fine, just a bit of play in the bearing, but it was ancient and the peace-of-mind factor was worth changing it. And, since it's not a tii, water pumps are short money. Lastly, I would've felt better if the car's aftermarket electric fuel pump had a spare. That one I *would* just throw in the trunk. Trivial, right?

But, in addition to these things, Bertha appeared to have some concerning driveline issues. Four separate ones, actually. They didn't sound like much, but collectively they felt like a big fat tether on my hitting the road.

The first was that the Getrag 245 5-speed was *really* noisy. It had what sounds like a gear whine when you got on it in any gear, and what sounded like a bearing rattle when you got off it in any gear. I had installed the 5-speed for Alex after I'd sold him the car. Neither he nor I have any memory of it behaving like this, and it's odd that either the theft event or the car's sitting would engender this behavior. I filled it with fresh Redline MTL and it made no difference. I thought about trying something heavier, like Swepco 201, but man that stuff is pricey. While I've never had a 2002 transmission detonate and leave me in the lurch, this one was loud enough that it raised that specter.

Figure 100: The Getrag 245 5-speed had some concerning issues.

Working backward from the transmission, the second issue was the giubo alignment problem that many 2002 5-speed conversions have. Because 02s didn't have 5-speed overdrive boxes when new, and because each conversion is different, it's common for the driveshaft to be misaligned with the giubo, prematurely shortening giubo life. When I put in the 5-speed for Alex in 1990, I installed everything Jim Rowe at The Metric Mechanic sent me, but alignment is more than just a matter of parts.

Figure 101: When the bolts are loose, seeing gaps between the giubo and the driveshaft flange is a sure sign of misalignment.

The hive mind at bmw2002faq believes that the goal should be to have the driveshaft and the giubo at a perfect right angle, so that the giubo isn't being distorted in any direction (in other words, ironically, so that the "flex disc" isn't being flexed). The way to achieve this is typically by adjusting the driveshaft center support bearing left, right, or down. It can't be adjusted upward, but if you needed it to be, you would instead adjust the back of the transmission downward at the mount. I doubt that, 27 years ago or whenever I installed the 5-speed for Alex, I paid the kind of attention to giubo/driveshaft alignment that people pay now. When I reinstalled Bertha's driveshaft after replacing her cracked giubo and lightly-binding center support bearing, I had to drop the CSB laughably low in order to even come close to alignment. Normally one would try raising the back of the transmission instead, but Bertha has an über-rare Metric Mechanic transmission bracket, and with it, the height of the back of the transmission isn't as adjustable as it is with the more common U-shaped bracket.

Figure 102: The center support bearing needed a laughable number of washers to shim it down.

The third issue was that, although the prevailing wisdom is that the alignment of the front half of the driveshaft with the giubo is more critical than the alignment of the front half of the driveshaft with the back half (everyone now ignores the fact that the 2002 factory manual dutifully shows how driveshaft alignment is achieved using two blocks of wood and a straightedge), if the driveshaft is cocked past a certain point, it *will* vibrate. I believed that some of that was occurring in Bertha.

Lastly, there was some low-speed noise that, when I had the car on the lift, appeared to be coming from the differential. I tried to change the fluid, but the fill plug stripped, despite my pre-heating it nearly cherry red, tapping in the Allen key socket, and hitting it with the impact wrench (always loosen the fill plug before removing the drain plug for exactly this reason). Unlike transmissions, I certainly *have* had differentials blow up on me. I did have other 2002 differentials, so I thought that, at some point, I should just take a few hours and swap one of them in and see what happens.

Figure 103: In addition to the transmission issues, the differential seemed to be a little noisy.

Together, the four of these issues comprised what I sometimes think of as "inertia repairs." That is, I continued to use the car for short trips without fixing them, but in order to address them, I needed to put an uncertain but likely substantial amount of effort into them, and the outcome, unless I wanted to spend a lot of money (e.g, new transmission) was unclear. Rather than do the repairs, it was easier to restrict the envelope of the use of the car. On paper, it didn't sound like much (other than the transmission itself), but every time I drove the car and either sped up or took my foot off the gas, the total effect was a rumbling whining or rumbling *beware*.

I thought I'd probably spend the eighty bucks, try the Swepco, swap the differential, make another stab at aligning the giubo, and see where that put me before sailing too far from shore. Bertha wanted to go somewhere. And I wanted to let her. I just didn't want her to come home at the end of a tow hook.

It all made sense, but one word came to my mind: Wimp.

In early September, just after Labor Day, the BMW CCA Vermont chapter event OktoberFAST was happening up in Burlington. On paper, it seemed like a good possible destination for a first road trip. It looked like close to 500 miles round trip—a stretch, but certainly not impossible if I wasn't, you know, a wimp.

I reconsidered. I took Bertha for a quick spin around the block. Nope, I thought; this doesn't feel right. This feels like something will go *BANGwobblewobblewobble* eighty miles south of Burlington. As I wrote in my first book, I often recall the Star Trek parable of the brave Klingon warrior who stays outside when a ferocious sandstorm is approaching. He says he is not afraid. He dies. Moral: The wind does not respect a fool. I try not to be a fool. That sometimes means being a wimp. But an *informed* wimp. Totally different.

However, as a writer who fixes cars, I sometimes become fixated on the idea that I can change the ending to a story, make it right by applying the correct combination of sweat, parts, ingenuity, and risk, and change *wimp* to *cool dude*. So even though my left brain said "don't do it," I badly wanted to write a column that began "Well, I ignored all my own advice, and Bertha and I blasted up I93 to I89 to Burlington, all 'tude and big-ass rust blisters and unburned hydrocarbons, went to OktoberFAST, Bertha was awesome, and everyone loved both of us because we are so cool."

That didn't happen.

But something pretty amazing *did* happen.

There's nothing reading like one's own punch list to get one moving. So, I winced, sighed, and ordered the $80/gallon Swepco 80W90 gear oil, thinking that, for that price, it'd better god damn have baby seal tears in it. And then I prepared to do the next thing on the list—swap the diff.

First, I performed some household archaeology and unearthed a spare differential. Amazingly, I believe it originally came from the same 2002ti that Bertha's front struts and brakes came from. The spare diff had been sitting under my mother's front porch for over 30 years before I finally moved it and some other parts over to my house in Newton a few years back. Then it sat under *my* porch. (I like to think of this as "seasoning.") I spun it to check that it was munch and rumble-free, cleaned it off, verified that it was stamped "40 11," giving it a 3.64 ratio, then made sure that neither the fill plug nor the drain plug were seized.

Next, I put Bertha on the lift, and did some forensics to be certain that the diff really was noisy. While driving the car, it certainly sounded like there was one set of noises—the whine and the rumble when on and off the gas—coming from the transmission, and a distinct light rumble coming from the rear of the car, audible when coasting at low speed in neutral. Sure enough, with the car in the air, the engine loafing at idle, and the transmission in second gear, there was a clearly audible rumble from the back of the car (you can find it on YouTube by searching for "Bertha noisy diff"). Of course, rumbles are notorious for telegraphing their way through a car, and even when underneath it, it's not easy to isolate a rumble to the differential as opposed to the half-axles or the rear wheel bearings.

If a differential is low on fluid, it will almost certainly be noisy. But I didn't *know* this diff was low on fluid. As I said, the diff's fill plug was seized so badly that I couldn't get it out, so there wasn't any way to check the fluid level or fill it with the diff in the car. Of course, I could undo the drain plug and see how much came out, but with no way to refill it, there was little point.

The best way to isolate rumbles is with a mechanic's stethoscope, but the entropy in my garage swallowed mine, so instead I held a hose to my ear, with the other end pointed at various components. The sound seemed to be coming from the right side of the rear end. I didn't feel any play in the right half-axle, but to be certain it wasn't the cause, I disconnected the right half-axle from the differential's flange and ran the car in gear. The noise lessened substantially. I swapped the half-axle with a spare. The noise came right back. I supposed it could've been the right wheel bearing. I removed the half-axle entirely and spun the right wheel. Nothing. Hmmmn.

I theorized that the differential was behaving differently when there was a torsional load on it and when there wasn't. It wasn't a 100% clear-cut "Yes, this differential is bad," but swapping a diff isn't that big of a deal, especially if you have a lift, a floor jack, a compressor, and an impact wrench, so rather than wondering about it, I just went ahead and did it.

I discovered, though, that I'd positioned Bertha inconveniently on the mid-rise lift. There are certain orientations where the differential is over part of the base of the lift, making it so that you can't roll a floor jack directly beneath the diff, and this was one of them. I had to skooch the front of the floor jack up onto the angled legs of the lift. It was a little hairy, but workable.

Figure 104: I remembered swapping a differential as easy. As one gets older, one is thankful for mechanical aids.

Out came the old diff. Out of curiosity, I drained it. Only about a cup of fluid came out, much less than the 1.5 quart fill capacity. That explained a lot. I suppose I could've filled it through the drain plug and re-installed it, but I already had the other one ready to go.

I filled the replacement differential and balanced it on the jack. Installing it required a bit of care, as it was difficult to position the floor jack accurately due to the interference from the base of the lift. I marveled that I used to lie on a creeper, put a differential on my chest, roll beneath a car, bench-press the thing into place, and hold it there with one elbow-locked arm while threading bolts in place with my other hand. Even using the lift, the whole thing was a lot harder than I remembered. I wondered what portion of that was my fading upper body strength, and what portion was my fading memory.

But in it went. I snugged down the bolts, fired up the engine, put the car in second gear, and smiled as the low-speed rumbling noise was gone. Bliss. (Search YouTube for "Bertha swapped differential.")

But that's not the amazing part.

As I said at the beginning of this chapter, I'd diagnosed four separate driveline issues with Bertha. The low-speed rumbling in neutral from the diff was only one of them. The car still had a transmission that whined badly when you got on the gas, and rumbled badly when you got off it. And munched 4th gear. My decision to blow eighty bucks on Swepco was a hail-Mary pass at trying to quiet the thing down.

The Swepco wasn't due to arrive until the end of the week. Bertha was already on the lift. My E9 coupe (the 3.0CSi) was behind it. Rain was forecast for the next few days. The lazy part of me and the part that likes to keep the 3.0 out of the rain both thought that I should just leave Bertha on the lift so when the Swepco arrived, I could drain the transmission, pump the Swepco in, and see what the result was. But the rational part of me thought that, if I did that, I wouldn't know what part of the problem the diff swap solved and what part was due to the baby seal tears in the Swepco, but it was really little more than an academic argument. I was confident that could distinguish transmission noises that were coming from right next to me from differential noises that were coming from the rear of the car.

Laziness and E9-related moisture fear won. I decided I'd leave the car on the lift and wait for the Swepco.

But the next day, the rain unexpectedly cleared. I moved the E9 out of the way, took Bertha down off the lift, and drove her.

To my stunned surprise and delight, with the differential swapped, the whining and rumbling when on and off the gas were completely gone. I was dead wrong about their origin. They were never coming from the transmission at all—they were coming from the rear end. You can witness my astonishment by searching YouTube for "First drive in Bertha with swapped diff."

There was still a light vibration that could be giubo or driveshaft-related. And the 5-speed still munched going into 4th gear. You could ease it in on upshift, but when rowing from 5th to 4th, as one needs to do with a 2002 5-speed on the highway, if you didn't double-clutch and match RPMs perfectly, it offered up a loud nasty metallic crunch.

But at the gut level, Bertha felt ready to go somewhere. And I felt ready to let her.

Anyone wanna buy a gallon of Swepco?

The Clutch Performance

As September 2018 settled into New England, I turned my gaze and wrenches to Bertha in a final push of fall fixes.

The big outstanding issue was Bertha's clutch hydraulics. The clutch master, as far as I know, was original to the car. I'd replaced the clutch slave when I'd installed the 5-speed, but that was probably in 1990. Regardless, the clutch hydraulics had sat for 26 years. Given that, my experience told me that clutch hydraulic failure was a near-certainty. It wasn't a question of if, but when, and how inconvenient it would be. So I ordered a new master and slave cylinder.

But with Bertha's whine-and-rumble vanquished, with New England's glorious September weather beckoning, and with the clutch stubbornly still working, I kept driving the car, albeit with the sword of clutch-Damocles dangling over its, uh, clutch. I was itchy for at least a mini-road-trip, so I took Bertha on a 150-mile round-trip drive up to New Hampshire and back to look at a well-priced E30 325is. The drive was nearly all highway, so shifting was minimal, but when I did need to shift, I noticed that the clutch pedal occasionally felt a little floppy, with most of the action near the bottom. Clearly, clutch hydraulic replacement time was drawing nigh. The new master cylinder, however, hadn't yet arrived.

A few days later, I received an e-mail from longtime Boston CCA chapter member John Whetstone inviting me to an informal event at the A&W drive-in burger joint in Smithfield, Rhode Island. I thought it sounded perfect for another mini-road trip in Bertha. John, who remembered Bertha from chapter events in the mid-80s, was excited about my bringing the car. With signs that Bertha's clutch hydraulics were teetering on the edge, I vacillated on taking her, but, like the drive up to New Hampshire, I figured that the 100-ish mile Rhode Island jaunt was mostly highway, and thought that would minimize the risk of the clutch hydraulics failing on the way. Plus, if need be, one can always start a car in gear, get it running, and shift by matching RPMs as best as one can. Bertha's transmission already has a destroyed 4th gear synchro; it's not like I'd be risking a pristine gearbox. The final part of my rationalization was that it was only Rhode Island; it's not like I was heading off into the great dark unknown. If the car croaked, AAA or Hagerty Roadside Assistance could drag it back at minimal cost. In the end, as Doc says in *Back to the Future,* "Sometimes you just have to say, 'what the hell.'" So on a crisp September evening, off Bertha and I went to Rhode Island for a burger and some BMW love.

But on the drive down, I hit unexpected traffic. I had to row 2nd to 3rd to 4th endlessly. Each time, I imagined the clutch pedal dropping to the floor like a puppet whose strings had been cut. Fortunately, the hydraulics soldiered on, I arrived at the A&W without incident, and had a great time. In addition to John Whetstone, other longtime Boston chapter members Joe Chamberlain, Mike Cinnamon, and Bruce Machon were there. It felt like old times. And Bertha was the center of attention, at least until Eric May arrived with his pristine 1970 Agave 2002, and a young man rolled in in a Polaris 850i six-speed with a black interior.

Figure 105: Bertha's orange Recaro fabric and rusty-patina-soaked hood looked right at home in the orange motif of the A&W.

As the event was winding down, Bruce Machon said that a bunch of folks were going to a pub to hear a great local blues band, and asked me if I wanted to come with them. I demurred. I was about to explain that I'd tempted fate enough with Bertha's clutch, but Bruce immediately said, in his deep Rhode Island baritone, "No, you're coming!" Right, then, I thought; I'm coming. It was a longer-than-anticipated drive to get to the pub, adding maybe another 20 miles round-trip. When we arrived and I parallel-parked Bertha, the transmission went in and out of gear without crunching, but clutch pedal definitely felt flaccid, requiring pumping to gain efficacy. I hoped I'd be able to pull her back out of the spot.

The band *was* great, but the evening and clutch-related anxiety began to catch up with me. I left, fired Bertha up, pumped up the clutch pedal, made a wish, put her in gear, backed her up, pulled forward out of the spot, and drove home, shifting as infrequently as possible. I made it with no issues. I put Bertha in the garage, positioned her over the lift, and tucked the E9 in behind her.

The next morning, the new clutch master cylinder arrived. All right then, I thought; I've tempted fate long enough. Let's get this done right now. I went out to the garage and moved the E9 out of the way, then noticed that I'd parked Bertha the wrong way over the lift. I needed to turn her around so her nose was forward, giving the greatest amount of room to work with all the crap in the garage.

I got in, hit the clutch, and the pedal went right to the floor.

I pumped it up a few times, and the pedal firmed up. I started the car, but when I tried to shift into gear, it just crunched.

The clutch hydraulics had officially failed. In my garage. Their replacement was no longer prophylactic.

I shut the car off, made sure there wasn't anything behind it, put it in reverse, and started it. The car did that ungainly *geHAWgeHAWgeHAW* thing it does when you unintentionally start it in gear, only this time it was intentional. The ignition soon caught, and I backed the car out of the driveway. The pedal pumped up just enough for me to put it in first. Rather than do a three-point turn to turn it around, I drove the car around the block. With a crunch, I got it in reverse, backed it into the garage, and maneuvered into the proper position over the lift. I hit the clutch pedal to take it out of gear, and the pedal again went right to the floor. I eased the gearshift into neutral so I wouldn't crash into the back wall of the garage.

Guess I got the maximum lifetime out of *those* clutch hydraulics, huh?

As I said earlier, I'm comfortable throwing a spare electric fuel pump in the trunk and swapping it on the road if the 33-year-old-one dies, but clutch hydraulics are best done in the comfort of your own garage. Most of the work is done under the car, so at a minimum, the car must be jacked up and securely supported. On a 2002 with a stock four-speed, the slave is mounted in a hole in the rim of the bell housing, held in place by two snap-rings that can be maddeningly challenging to remove, and even once you get them off, the steel slave can be rust-welded into the aluminum hole in the bell housing due to corrosion of dissimilar metals, requiring relentless heating-and-beating to get it out. These issues were all in play a year and a half prior when I had to deal with Louie's clutch hydraulics in Louisville. Fortunately, Bertha wasn't as recalcitrant. She has a Getrag 245 five-speed on which the slave is bolted to the side. The upper slave nut requires a long extension and a wobble joint to reach it, but other than that, the slave is easy to replace.

Figure 106: There's not much clearance for the slave on a 2002 5-speed, but it can be removed and installed without major headache.

The master cylinder, though, is more of a pain. To remove it, the attachment point to the clutch pedal must be accessed in the pedal bucket from inside the car. This requires peeling back the rug. On a '73 or earlier 2002 with a multi-piece rug, this is trivial, but on a big-bumpered car with a one-piece rug and air conditioning, it can be a major pain, as part of the rug is usually trapped on the hump by the console and evaporator assembly. Fortunately I'd anticipated this issue when I rebuilt the air conditioning, and made certain not to screw the evaporator bracket into the rug.

When I unbolted the clutch pedal from the master cylinder, I found a small issue—the two nylon bushings on the pivot bolt were worn out. This explained the play and squeaking in the clutch pedal. I put a pair of bushings on order at my local BMW dealer ($1.74 each) and had them in a day.

Figure 107: The old (left) and new (right) clutch pivot bushings.

The clutch master cylinder itself is bolted through the pedal bucket, with two 13mm bolt heads on the inside and two 13mm nuts under the car. There are two challenges to removing it. The first is that someone, or something, has to hold the bolt heads still while someone undoes the nuts, or vice versa. On the Louie adventure, someone #2 was my friend Dave Gerwig, who stuck with me through cold and darkness and held a flashlight and a wrench in Jake Metz's then-unelectrified pole barn to help me change Louie's clutch master when it failed as I was about to hit the highway home. With Bertha safely moored in the comfort of my own garage, though, doing this without a helper was pretty straightforward; it merely involved positioning a wrench, or a socket and handle, so that, when the nut or bolt was loosened from the other side, the wrench swung and caught on something solid. (You can also hold the bolt in place with a vise-grip.)

The second issue is that the top nut on the master cylinder is difficult to turn or hold still. Due to clearance issues, you can't get either a socket or a box-end wrench on it. Some folks use a short open-end wrench. I used the same crow foot wrench I bought at a Harbor Freight in Louisville to get the master off Louie. At that time, I'd held the crow foot in place with a ratchet handle and extension while Dave loosened the bolt from inside the car, but on Bertha, I found that if I slipped the crow foot over the top of the nut as pictured below, it rotated to the right and pinned itself in place when, from inside the car, I loosened the bolt.

Figure 108: The crow foot wrench pinned itself in place and held the upper nut still while I loosened the bolt from inside the car.

I've read about how, prior to installation of a new clutch master, folks grind a little bit off the cylinder's lip to get clearance for a socket or wrench, but I left it the way it was and used the crow foot again to hold the nut for installation.

The other thing you need to know about the clutch master installation is that you need to seat the metal or plastic rigid line from the brake fluid reservoir into the rubber grommet in the master *before* you install the master in the car. This means disconnecting the line from the reservoir, holding it in one hand and the master in the other, and pushing and twisting the line into the grommet to seat it. You might think that you can do this with the master installed in the pedal bucket, but it is nearly impossible to get the proper angle and enough leverage.

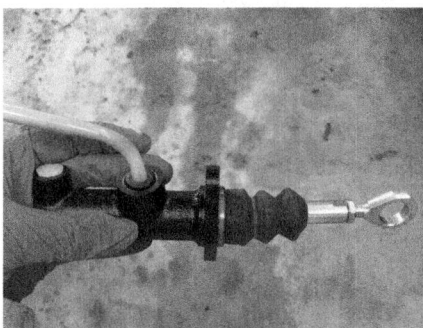 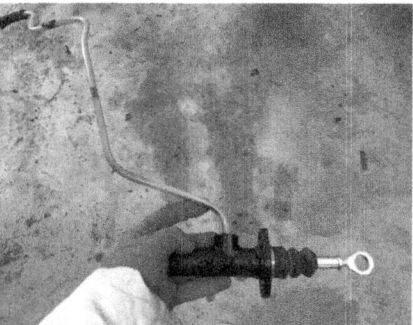

Figure 109: The hydraulic line has to be first installed in the grommet, and then the pipe and clutch master cylinder installed together.

Once the line is seated, you then install the master and line together. You can do this from above (lowering the master in place) or below (snaking the rigid line upward). If you do it from above, the technique—and I'm going to quote my friend Paul Wegweiser directly—is "lowering the master cylinder into place by the line as if you're dangling a chicken neck to a bunch of snapping turtles."

The only remaining issue was the flexible clutch hose that connects the master cylinder to the slave. 5-speeds need a longer hose than the stock 4-speed. Bertha's existing clutch hose was seized in both the slave and master; the corners of their 11-mm nuts rounded off even when I was using a flare-nut wrench after applying heat and wax. Re-using the existing hose would've been false economy anyway. Several specialty vendors (Ireland, La Jolla, Rogers Tii) sell a purpose-built 2002 5-speed braided clutch hose with two male ends at the correct angles. I almost bought one, but then recalled that I had a braided stainless clutch line of some sort in the garage. I found it, saw that it had a female fitting at one end, ran down to Autozone to buy a short male-to-male metric bubble fitting line to mate to it, bent the metal line to not interfere with the upper nut on the clutch slave, and installed it.

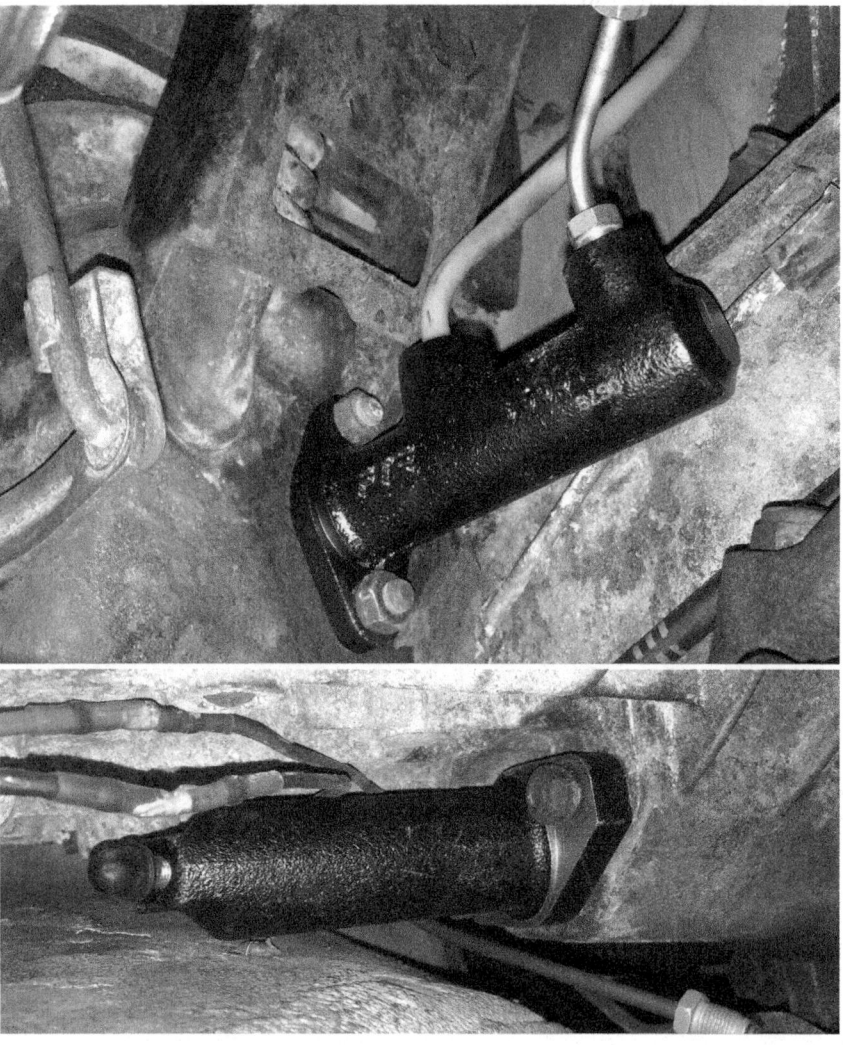

Figure 110: The newly-installed clutch master and slave with their metal lines attached.

So, the clutch hydraulics were finally done, and there were some crucial spares in Bertha's trunk. That left just one completely frivolous thing.

The Facelift and Butt Tuck

For the 28-ish years that my friend Alex owned Bertha, he talked about doing a bumper conversion—replacing her U.S.-spec bridge-abutment bumpers with the small thin chrome bumpers it would've had if it was a Euro car. I didn't really understand the appeal. If you want small bumpers, I always thought, buy a round tail light 2002; don't go to extraordinary effort to create this odd American-European hybrid. After all, if you merely swap the bumpers, you're still stuck with the U.S.-spec side-marker lights (plainly visible in the corners of the fenders of the photo above). Part of the appeal of the Euro look is that it is holistic; the entire car appears not only smaller and trimmer, but without the side-marker lights, it also looks smoother. The bumper conversion only gets you partway there.

However, as it turned out, Alex was ahead of his time. So-called "small-bumpered squaries" became a big thing. Initially, each of them was home-rolled, with the conversion requiring non-trivial fabrication of bumper brackets. At some point, though, an enterprising guy named Eric Anton began selling bumper bracket kits on bmw2002faq.com.

Recently, BMW parts vendor BluntTech began selling a similar kit. So these days, you can procure front and rear bumpers, buy one of these two bracket kit, drill a few holes in the rear quarter panels to attach the "ears" on the curved corner pieces, tighten a few bolts, and you're done. At least in theory.

But even with kits available, I had zero interest in doing the bumper conversion on Bertha. Small bumpers weren't something I lusted after for the car anyway; they were Alex's dream, not mine. I'm a pragmatist, and after all, the car needed mountains of work in order to get it running, then drivable, then sorted. A bumper swap seemed utterly frivolous. Plus, so much of Bertha's history and image were embodied in those big bumpers. As I've said, I bought Bertha in Austin in 1984 when Maire Anne and I knew we'd be returning to Boston; I actually *wanted* a big-bumpered '02 to stand up to Boston traffic and parking. Her very name "Bertha" originated from the fact that, with those battering ram bumpers, she was anything but dainty. And, although in her present resurrected incarnation, I'll be unlikely to rely on the big bumpers to, say, parallel park her regularly on the streets of Cambridge, those bumpers, especially the front one supporting the two giant Cibié Oscar driving lights, were an inextricable part of her vibe.

Figure 111: A face only a father could love: That giant battering ram of a bumper and those big lights certainly gave Bertha a certain, uh, presence. You can see in this photo how the bumper was pushed in on the right, a fact that became significant during its replacement.

But then a few things happened. First, understand that, even though I am now Bertha's owner (again), Alex and I both think of her as "our car." And that's appropriate. After all, as I've said, we first met in 1984 because I drove Bertha, with her driver's door missing, into his shop, and I asked if I could borrow a door. The replacement for the door he didn't have is still in primer to this day, an immediate visual reminder of that meeting whenever either of us sees the car. Alex took a longer road trip in Bertha than I ever did; I loaned it to him and his first wife Heidi so they could take a six-week "Grand Circle" swing through national parks for their honeymoon. And, technically, he owned the car for longer than I did, though for most of his ownership, the car was dead and off the road because it got stolen, vandalized, hit lightly, and appeared to have had its engine damaged.

I noticed that, in my continued conversations with Alex, the issue of the bumper conversion he never got to do kept coming up. I initially brushed this off as just the tip of the iceberg of Alex's pie-in-the-sky vision for a ground-up restoration that was never likely to happen. But the more that I thought about it, the more I realized that it fit with what I was trying to do with Bertha. In resurrecting her, I was trying to be true to her heritage, to how I'd built her in the mid-80s with parts ordered from *Roundel* magazine advertisers, plus doing a few mods that I never got to do back in the day such as 14" silver E30 steel wheels (which I'm still looking for). It began to feel right to extend that heritage to include the small bumpers that Alex had always wanted to install. More than that, the bumper conversion was the intersection of Alex's visionary tendencies and my more practical incremental ones. I didn't have the money or the time to restore the car (which made no sense anyway), but a small bumper conversion, *that* I could do.

Second, a few years back, I'd bought a bunch of parts from a body shop that was getting out of the vintage BMW restoration business. The hoard included a dozen 2002, E3, and E9 bumpers. The best ones got sold immediately. The remaining ones weren't in great shape, and they lingered, unwanted and unloved, in the backyard for months. Maire Anne, who asks very little of me, gently requested that I remove them. I stashed them in the back of the storage spaces I have out in Fitchburg. A few months ago, I literally tripped on the bumpers while moving around the cars. I saw that I had still had three 2002 front bumpers which, collectively, had all necessary un-dented sections—the long center piece, the two curved end pieces with the ears for the fender bolts, and the two bumperettes (overriders)—with relatively intact chrome. The best bumperettes were missing the thick rubber pads, but the pads on the worst bumperettes, the ones that were too bent and rusty to consider for use even on Bertha, were good. It seemed that, if I mixed and matched,

I could make one pretty good front bumper, though I still needed to procure a rear one (I kicked myself for having sold three good ones).

Figure 112: For a time, the backyard was bumper central.

Lastly, the proceeds from the books that I write and publish go into a PayPal account. It's essentially automotive mad money. Although I will frequently go to ridiculous often pound-foolish lengths to save the last dollar on parts purchases, every once in a while I'll use this account to buy something frivolous. Like parts for a small bumper conversion.

So, one night in mid-September 2018, I saw that Bertha's punch list of mechanical issues had gotten quite short, and felt that the bumper conversion would be a nice cherry on the sundae of the whole resurrection project. I searched for information on Eric Anton's bumper brackets on bmw2002faq.com (they're often referred to as "the Anton brackets") and found that people liked them; they were reportedly easy to install and the results looked good. I found his contact information and asked him about cost and delivery. Yes, he said, he still sold them. Yes, the price was still $260 shipped. No, they weren't "in stock," as each set was fabricated when ordered; it'd take about a week. I dipped into the mad money and ordered the brackets from Eric.

Bertha was going to get the facelift and butt-tuck that Alex always wanted to give her.

Some folks have asked me why I ordered the Anton brackets instead of the kit from BluntTech. To be absolutely clear about this, at the time, I didn't know that BluntTech had a kit; they'd just recently begun selling it. So don't read anything at all into my choice. From what I can tell, the two kits appear to be quite similar. They both have brackets that slide into the holes vacated by the old bumpers' hydraulic cylinders, and bolt to the back sides of the smaller chrome bumpers. They both provide "pre-2 1/2 mph" bumper spacing where the rear bumper is flush against the body and the front bumper is slightly forward of the tip of the hood. They both work with all three front bumper configurations (upright bumperettes like a '72 or earlier, pointy bumperettes like a '73, or no bumperettes like a Euro) and the two different rear bumpers (long-eared and "shorty," each with and without bumperettes). They both come with a clear piece of Plexiglass to cover up the extra space where the brackets go through the nose; you're supposed to paint it the body color and affix to the nose with adhesive. The major difference is that Blunt's front brackets are each a single piece, whereas Anton's are two-piece, using an intermediate piece that bolts onto the bumper and then onto the bracket. Other differences are that BluntTech's pieces are powder-coated rather than painted, BluntTech claims that their metal is heavier gauge (I have not verified this), and, shipped, the BluntTech kit costs about $60 more than the Anton kit.

Figure 113: The front bumper pieces of the Anton bracket kit. Fasteners and Plexiglass covers not shown.

While I waited for the kit to arrive, I procured a rear bumper. And that in itself is a story that I feel privileged to tell.

In 2011, I wrote a *Roundel* magazine column titled *Saving 2590507* about my winding up with a Verona '73 2002 that was owned by a young woman named Erica, daughter of my friend Brad, who was Alex's former business partner. Erica's 2002 had a Momo Mario Andretti steering wheel in it that originally came from a '73 tii I'd traded to Brad for some work on my mother's house in the mid-1980s. Before I sold Erica's car, I snagged the steering wheel, replacing it with an old bus wheel I had. I couldn't even say why. I didn't install it into anything. I guess I just loved the history it represented. Eight years later, when I bought Bertha back, I was surprised to find her wearing an original padded bus wheel. I would've laid money that, with the car's myriad of mods, surely I would've installed something sportier. Maybe I did. Maybe Alex changed it back. I'm not certain. But the Momo Andretti wheel went on Bertha, and instantly felt like it'd always been there.

In *Saving 2590507*, I also relayed the remarkable story about the engine in Erica's car that was told to me by my Nor'East 02'er friend Wink Cleary, who'd sold the engine to Brad and Erica years back. The engine came from a parts car that Wink had gotten from an elderly gentleman. Wink says: "He told me the car had been his son's baby. His son was killed in the first Iraq war. His wife learned to drive a stick so she could drive the '02; it made her feel still connected to their son. She drove it back and forth to work every day until it collapsed onto its rear axles. They parked it in front of the trailer and she touched it on her way out every morning. When she died, he wanted to find a good home for what was way more than a car to him. He said I could have it so it wouldn't just get crushed." Given the story, I always imagined that, if the soldier's parents could've heard their son's engine run in Erica's car, they would've been moved by the automotive version of hearing a transplanted heart beating in someone else's chest.

I think about things like this—Bertha's steering wheel, Erica's engine—and how all that nuance, all that history gets erased when a car is sold. Even if you tell the new buyer, it's just never going to have the same import. The components will just be interchangeable parts to him or her.

I mention all this because, when I put out the call to the Nor'East 02'er Facebook page, it was Wink Cleary who responded, saying that he had a decent bumper from a round tail light car. After Wink sent me some photos and I'd made arrangements to pick it up, he said "You know where the bumper came from? The same car as Erica's motor."

Wow.

Knowing the history of Bertha's new rear bumper, every time I look at it, I feel moved that Bertha and I get to help a piece of a car, formerly owned by a soldier and 2002 enthusiast I never met, run around in the world.

The basic steps for both the front and rear bumper conversion are:

- Remove the big bumpers and their hydraulic cylinders. (Step one in the Anton kit's instructions literally says "REMOVE THOSE BIG ASS UGLY STOCK BUMPERS." I liked the kit immediately.)
- If you're installing a long rear bumper, remove the trim pieces behind the rear wheels, as they're in the way.
- Test-fit the bumper brackets in the car.
- Measure the distance between them accurately.
- Take the brackets out, mount them on the back of the small bumper, and adjust things so the spacing between the brackets is the same as when they were installed in the car.
- Use the supplied paper templates to mark where the new holes to attach the bumper ears should go.
- Drill those holes.
- If you like, fill the old holes where the accordion corner pieces of the big bumpers went.
- Mount, adjust, tighten.

Figure 114: Using the paper template that came with the Anton kit to mark the hole for the front bumper ear.

On Bertha, one of the most time-consuming parts of the project was the fact that I was mixing and matching to assemble good bumpers. Swapping rubber pads on the bumperettes was very problematic. You can buy these new for as low as about $32 before shipping, and that's what I should've done, but nnnnnnnooooooooo; I tried to hold costs down and re-use them from other bumpers. The problem is that they're held on to the bumperette by two 10mm nuts threaded onto M6 studs that are sunk into the rubber. After 45 years, the nuts are seized on the studs, and when you try to undo them, the backs of the studs just spin in the rubber, and there's basically no way to grab them and hold them still. If you're very careful, you can use a Dremel tool and a cutting wheel to cut off the seized nuts above the washers separating them from the back of the bumperette, leaving just enough thread to put a new nut on.

Figure 115: You're never going to be able to loosen the frozen 10mm nuts holding the rubber pads to the bumperettes.

I did the rear bumper first, inserting the brackets and test-fitting the bumper with no problems. I then drilled the holes for the ears, but noticed that there was some rust bubbling not only around the old holes for the accordion pieces, but also in other places that the big bumper had been hiding. Bertha is obviously a body-challenged car on which my sanding or not sanding these bubbles wasn't going to make a great deal of difference, but I hastily wire-wheeled the rust, sprayed on some rust-inhibiting primer, sealed the old holes with POR-15 Patch, called it good enough, and completed the installation.

I instantly loved the way the new rear bumper looked. I no longer have a ready-made shelf for my beer when standing around the back of the car, but I can live with that.

Figure 116: Bertha's rear bumper changed from this...

Figure 117: ...to this.

I next removed Bertha's front bumper, and had to laugh at how the bellows surrounding the hydraulic cylinders had deteriorated into circular black rings that looked like calamari.

Figure 118 This kind of calamari takes 43 years to prepare.

Before I began the process of assembling a Frankenstein's monster of a front bumper, I entertained using a straight but rusty one I had with no bumperettes on it. After all, its rust was nearly a perfect match to Bertha's heavily-patina'd hood. I hung the bumper briefly on the brackets. It had a certain appeal, but the idea of installing a rusty bumper when I could build a clean one seemed wrong. Also, while I am extremely enamored of Bertha's patina, the way her rusty hood tells the story of her 26 years in captivity, I'm not looking to crank her rat-rod-ness up to 11 or turn her into a rusty joke, and intentionally attaching a rusty bumper grazed uncomfortably close to that line.

Figure 119: I thought about using this rusty bumper, but backed off.

The front bumper installation proved much more troublesome than the rear. It was clear that during Bertha's theft 26 years ago, she hit something; the original front bumper was slightly pushed in on the right and there was a dent in the right front fender. I expected that to cause a problem affixing the bumper's right ear. However, when I removed the bumper and test-fit the brackets, it was immediately obvious that there was a bigger problem: The right bracket was toed substantially inward. When I looked in the engine compartment, I could see that the root cause was that the right bumper support—the extension of the right frame rail—was noticeably bent. I wondered if this was going to drag the whole swap to a halt.

Figure 120: You can see how the right bracket (left in photo) is cocked inward.

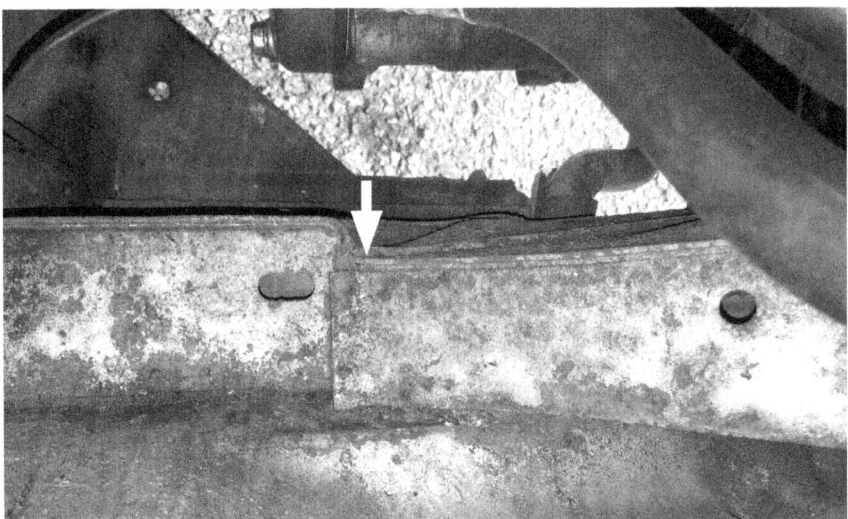

Figure 121: The right front bumper support was clearly buckled where it attached to the frame rail.

There's an expression that you often hear in business and politics: Don't let the perfect be the enemy of the good. As a mechanic, I get a lot of mileage out of this approach. Here I was, fitting bumpers on a car that looked like it had passed through lava. I wasn't going to let the process get train-wrecked by a buckled bumper support.

Each front bumper bracket is held in place by a big bolt at its rear and a smaller positioning bolt near its front. I inserted the bolt at the rear but left the front bolt out, and slid the front of the bracket as far over as it would go to try to toe it outward. I then test-fit the bumper and marked where I'd need to drill a new hole in the bracket for the front bolt. Rather than follow the instructions and remove the brackets, bolt them to the bumper, and set the spacing at a pre-determined amount, instead I attached the bumper to the already-inserted brackets, and took turns tightening all of the bolts. In this way, I was able to get the bumper to fit adequately considering the rest of the challenging aspects of the car's exterior.

Even though I included a photo above of the hole template, I didn't wind up drilling any new holes for the front bumper. With the alignment already imperfect due to the accident, I found that one of the existing holes from where the side bellows mounted was close enough. And I didn't use the Plexiglass pieces to cover the gaps around where the brackets went through the nose because Bertha's nose is too dented to have those pieces sit flush against it.

Note that, because the BluntTech bumper kit has one-piece front bumper brackets, it's possible that it may be a little less work for most people to use, but the fact that the Anton kit has two-piece front bumper brackets may have given me some extra play and adjustability that helped me with my bent front bumper support.

As I was installing the front bumper, I realized two things. The first was that I was missing the small irregularly-shaped aluminum spacers that sit between the bumper bracket and the inside of the bumper. I substituted stacks of washers, which worked well enough. The second was that the '72 and earlier upright bumperettes I had gave the car a slightly flat-faced look. I put out the call on Facebook to see if anyone had the spacers and '73-style pointy bumperettes. I thought about waiting until I had these parts, but with the number of cars and projects I have, I make no apologies for the fact that I sometimes tailor the level of effort of a repair to make it fit into the time allotted. I may revisit the spacers and bumperettes at a later date, but it was done, and that's what it needed to be.

Figure 122: Here's Bertha pre-facelift...

Figure 123: And here she is with the bandages off.

With the new bumpers, Bertha's overall appearance was much trimmer, and her new nose certainly looked neat and tidy. Although I liked it a lot, I wasn't quite as bowled over by the look of the new front bumper as I was the rear. I guess that's understandable. The front of a car is its face, and with the loss of both the bumper and the big Cibié Oscar driving lights, it was a big change. I thought that, at some point, I'd install the beautiful set of vintage Cibié Oscars my friend Alan Hunter Johansson sent me, and that might restore some of the swagger to Bertha's nose. And maybe swap the bumperettes for those from a '73.

But perhaps more important was Alex's reaction. I showed him the face-lifted car before anyone else saw it. He looked at it, smiled, sighed, and said quietly "I always wanted to do that." I know, Alex. I know.

And now, every time I see a photo of a stock square tail light 2002, I stare at it and think *"damn* those bumpers are big!"

Still, it could be worse. At about this time, BMW released the first press photos of the new X7 and its monstrously large front grille. Book designer Eric King had some fun in Photoshop and imagined what it might look like on Bertha.

Figure 124: At least Bertha didn't look like this.

Adding Up the Costs

When I agreed to buy back Bertha from Alex back in June 2018, I wrote that there is no universe in which the purchase makes any financial sense whatsoever, and that I was buying her back because there is only one car in which Maire Anne and I drove off from our wedding, and it's this one. But with my modest income as a writer, I wanted to be careful not to dump stupid money into the car.

Bertha's appearance is certainly, um, how to put it... striking. You can't possibly miss the hood that looks like acid was dripped on it, and the driver's door that's been in primer since 1984. And if you look more closely, you can see dents and small bits of surface rust on every body panel. Folks often ask if I'm going to paint it, and are surprised when I answer in the negative.

Most non-car people don't have a clue regarding what's involved in painting a car. You don't do it without, at a minimum, addressing surface rust, visible rust holes, and dents. It would be like painting a house that was hit by a tree without first repairing the damage. I can't imagine that, even hunting for a bargain price, an outer body restoration on Bertha wouldn't instantly zoom to the multiple five figure mark. Plus, to me, Bertha is all about the story, and her distressed paint, the rust-scarred hood, and especially the door in primer, are all inextricable parts of that story. After all, as we get older, we wear *our* scars. Why shouldn't Bertha?

So, no, Bertha is *not* going to be painted.

I just saved myself twenty grand. Woo-*whoo*!

I joke, but the math was always simple. Paint Bertha = it doesn't make sense. Don't paint Bertha = well, I said there's not a universe in which buying back Bertha makes sense. Maybe it's not so simple. Scratch that.

Although I don't save pieces of papers in folders to the same degree that I used to, I will typically keep careful track of car expenses in a spreadsheet. If I bought a car with resale in mind, at some point I'll add the expenses up so I know what kind of headroom I have. But for a car like Louie or Bertha that I have no intention of selling, I'll often track the expenses but not add them up because, well, if I do, it's just too depressing.

Still, with Bertha, I needed to know exactly how stupid I'd been. I needed to know how much it had cost me to pull the trigger on this odd passion project and buy back and resurrect the car that I sold 30 years prior primarily because I no longer had the space to keep both it and the 3.0CSi, but also because I'd turned it into an over-modified hot rod, and, to be perfectly candid, the drove-off-from-my-wedding-in-it thing notwithstanding, I never really laid awake pining to have it back.

Here's how it shakes out.

Below are the non-discretionary costs to purchase, register, and inspect the car. (Well, the purchase was certainly discretionary, but you know what I mean.) I was enormously fortunate that, as I wrote about previously, I did not have to pay sales tax to the state of Massachusetts since I never technically relinquished ownership of the car (Alex had never legally registered it). In addition, Hagerty calculated that there was no additional incremental cost to adding it to my insurance policy.

Purchase	$ 1,500
Registration	$ 135
Inspection	$ 35
Subtotal	$ 1,670

Below is a list of all the parts I purchased while sorting out the car and getting it to the point where it was inspectable, then reliable. As anticipated, these total more than the costs to purchase the car and put it on the road, but not by much. It's also a very handy summary of what was involved in Bertha's resurrection. I'd again like to thank my friend Bob Sawtelle who gave me a set of his unused E30 basketweaves and correctly-sized 195/60/14 tires on long-term loan, freeing me from having to buy wheels and rubber.

exhaust resonator and brake rotors	$ 161
rear brakes and front pads	$ 142
head gasket set	$ 60
center support bearing	$ 24
calipers	$ 68
flexible lines	$ 80
misc nuts bolts clamps bushings	$ 66
machine shop valve job	$ 300
intake and exhaust valve	$ 47
correct intake valve	$ 37
valve guide	$ 23
correct valve guide	$ 28
clutch slave	$ 18
heater box fan	$ 62
fan belt	$ 8
spare water pump	$ 36
battery	$ 58
misc antifreeze oil headlights	$ 100
exhaust hangers	$ 10
speedometer cable	$ 40
redline mtl	$ 39
sway bar bushings	$ 15
windshield gasket	$ 130
windshield frame repair supplies	$ 35
POR15 seam sealer	$ 15
sandpaper	$ 12
second windshield	$ 100
fasteners	$ 7
horn spring and plunger	$ 20
dust caps for basketweaves	$ 20
alternator	$ 86
tighter belt	$ 10

swepco	$	76
spare fuel pump	$	14
hotspark ignition module	$	40
clutch master	$	60
gas tank level sensor o-ring	$	6
clutch metal line	$	5
subtotal	$	2,058

Below are the handful of items that were not strictly needed for sort-out, and were instead comfort or appearance-related.

recaro seat webbing	$	33
bumper bracket kit	$	260
rear bumper	$	75

Below are the air conditioning-specific items.

condenser	$	35
fan	$	86
expansion valve	$	30
a/c hoses, fittings, adapters	$	103
compressor head	$	25
compressor gasket set	$	11
flush	$	10
ester oil	$	13
two cans R134a	$	15
subtotal	$	328

If you add it all up, it comes to... a little under $4500. $4424 to be precise. Or, $3728 to buy her back and get her legal and running reliably, plus about another $800 for the non-essentials of working a/c and small bumpers.

Holy crap. If I saw Bertha advertised on Craigslist for that price, I'd be burning rubber to be the first in line with a pocket full of cash.

No? Not you? Just me? At that price, do you scratch your head and think "Gee, that drove-off-from-my-wedding-in-it drug must be wicked strong in New England?" That's fine.

I am not a wealthy man. I'm a person who makes choices. There are many things I could spend $4424 on. This one has brought me a lot of pleasure.

Figure 125: They say never to photograph a car with a tree growing through its roof. Except when the tree is October awesome and the car is Bertha.

I tend to go full-on things. I was full-on Bertha for about four and a half months. Then I bought a 1987 E28 535i (a.k.a. "The Lama," so-named for its Lama-colored (that's BMW's name) interior), and I began to deal with the fact that it was far needier than I expected, including having a broken rocker arm. I went full-on The Lama for months. So there were a few weeks in the fall of 2018 where Bertha sat, sporting her new bumpers but not going anywhere wearing them.

So, one evening in October 2018, I took her for a nice crisp evening spin. I first ripped off the packing tape that was closing off the flow of air from the heater box into the cabin. Part of the tape's purpose was to keep hot ambient air out during the summer, and part was because I was afraid the thing was going to bloody stink of dead rodent from Bertha's 26-year incarceration.

It was fine. The heat was clean-smelling and strong.

I did about twenty miles, just up I-95 a few exits and back down, nailing and wailing each time I came up the ramp. Bertha was running great. The myriad big and small things that I fixed add up to a damned fun car.

But then, as I got off the exit, I realized... I hadn't brought a single tool with me. No green-handled reversible slotted and Phillips screwdriver. No 10 and 13mm combination wrench. Nothing. Crikey, not even a voltmeter.

Bertha had made it. There *is* a universe where her resurrection made sense. As it happens, it's the one in which I live.

Part 3

Life After Resurrection

Garage Space, Revisited

In the introduction to this book, I talked about how it's challenging for folks of moderate means like me to hold onto cars because we're not well-heeled collectors; we don't have Garage Mahals or big metal outbuildings on our back 40 or rented industrial space or space associated with a business that we own. But I didn't say what sleight of hand I use that allows me to own, at present, 12 cars. To break it down, as of this writing, that's two daily drivers (my 2003 530i stick sport and Maire Anne's 2013 Honda Fit sport), the Winnebago Rialta RV (a VW Eurovan with a Winnebago camper body on it), the seven vintage BMWs (two '72 2002tiis, Bertha, a '73 Bavaria, the '73 3.0CSi I've owned since 1986, and a '79 Euro 635CSi), a '73 faux 2002tii parts car, a '99 Z3 M Coupe, and the long-dead '74 Lotus Europa Twin-Cam Special which will be the car that kills me, or at least, as Michael Roach joked years back, drives me to hobby desertion.

I'm not infrequently asked "So, if you say you're not rich and you don't rent a warehouse, where do you *put* 12 cars?" Well, the two daily drivers and the Rialta sit outside, as does the faux tii parts car, so we're not talking about garaging 12 cars year-round, only (he says sheepishly) eight. But even still, I don't have an eight-car garage.

The answer is: They're stored in multiple places. BMW CCA member Greg Menounos sent me a link to a PBS *Nature* piece on the squirrel, describing it as a "scatter hoarder." Greg thought that I'd see some of myself in the furry little critter. Well played, Greg; well played.

You have to understand that I didn't always have 12 cars. The number just kind of creeps up. Buying cars is a series of crimes of opportunity. If you see an ad on Craigslist for a rust-free '73 Bavaria in a warehouse in southern Maine for five grand, go look at the car, find that it really *is* honest-to-god rust-free, tell the buyer that you're interested but winter is coming and you have no space for it, have him say that you can leave it in his warehouse over the winter for a hundred bucks and by the way I know who you are I've been reading your stuff for years I'd love the car to go to you so for you, four grand… what are you supposed to do, *not* buy it? Do that and The Automotive Powers That Be will stop dangling cars in front of you. Repeat this three or four or five times and before you know it, you have a ridiculous unsupportable number of cars and don't want to part with any of them. Welcome to my freaking world.

Initially, I was a single-location hoarder. I can easily fit three cars in the garage at my house. To squeeze in another, I can put one car on wheel dollies and slide it sideways, allowing a fourth car to be pulled in, but for the past several years, the floor of the garage has been so overrun with boxes of parts (no, let me call it what it is: crap) that this is no longer possible. In addition, there's a sliding door on the garage's left wall that accesses another carport-like space under the deck that hangs off the kitchen, but that long ago got filled by the lawnmower, snow blower, Lotus parts, and other detritus of life. I still stash one car in the industrial space associated with my old geophysics job as part of a quid pro quo of my keeping a little-used work truck registered and inspected for them, but as the car numbers crept up, that wasn't enough.

Figure 126: What I can do in theory to fit four cars in the garage.

Figure 127: Why theory and practice aren't the same thing.

Garage space in suburban Boston costs, as I said earlier, about $300/month, and for that, you typically don't get private in-and-out-anytime-you-want space. You get half of someone's two-car garage, and they want you to roll the car in after Thanksgiving and roll it out on Memorial Day. I found, however, that as you look farther from Boston, rents drop off substantially. About five years back I read an ad for a $50-a-month garage space in Fitchburg, a little over 40 miles west of me, and drove out to see the space and meet the owner (Eddie). There were five spaces, each with its own roll-up door, in front of a house he was refurbishing. The spaces were small, but so are my cars; I wasn't planning on sticking a vintage fire truck or even a Suburban in any of them. The pluses were the low cost and 24-hour access, but the minuses were the distance from my house, the lack of electricity or heat, and some amount of dampness in the spaces.

"Is only one of these spaces available?" I asked.

"Right now, yes," replied Eddie.

"Contact me," I said, "when other spaces open up, because at that price, *I will rent all five.*"

Eddie and I developed a rapport, and learned that we were both people who were true to our word. He'd call me as spaces became available, I'd say, "Yes, I want them," and within eighteen months I was renting four of the five spaces for a total of $200 a month. This has worked out incredibly well. Although I'd prefer for all of my cars to be on the property or close by, that's simply not possible. And it certainly isn't hardship for me to jump in one vintage BMW on a Sunday morning, drive it for an hour, and swap it for another one. Along with Hagerty's almost laughably low insurance rates on my sub-$10,000 cars, the four spaces I rent in Fitchburg have been a major enabling factor allowing the number of cars to hover around the average age of audience members at a Taylor Swift concert.

So, what's at the house at any moment is a combination of what I'm working on and what I want to have around for fun. The long-dead Lotus (I actually *am* working on it again) occupies the space in the left rear corner of the garage. The mid-rise lift is in the space in the right rear corner, so that's for either whatever the active project is, or whatever has broken that has to be returned to service quickly. The space in the right front corner is in front of the roll-up door, so that's for whichever car is being actively driven. So, garage-wise, the process of resurrecting Bertha in the summer of 2018, getting her running, then reliable, was one in which she went from monopolizing the lift for months, to being on and off it, to being in the most-accessed garage spot (or in the driveway when the weather was good).

Once Bertha crossed over the line into well-sorted-land, I had a heavenly time with her. I loved having her at the house. She filled a gap in the other cars I didn't realize I had. Unlike my other 1970s BMWs which all have a somewhat refined sense about them, Bertha is raw, visceral, and snotty. I love the snarl the engine makes through the Webers and the feel of the go-cart-stiff suspension. During the fall of 2018, I drove her at every opportunity, whether it was to jump in her and run out for take-out, throw a guitar on the back seat and play a gig, or to do some corner-carving. It was absolutely addictive.

Then I bought The Lama, and wound up having to yank and rebuild its head. The Lama thus occupied the "project space" on the lift, and Bertha was there to help me de-stress by allowing me to hop in, drive, boot, and listen to the Webers scream.

I kept hoping that I'd be able to squeeze a road trip with Bertha in during the fall—Maire Anne and I even talked about recreating our Nova Scotia trip 30 years prior—but it was a busy few months, the weeks slipped by, and as the calendar turned over to December and we had the first snowfall, I needed to make some decisions regarding which cars would be where. Winter in New England is fickle. A month can go by when the temperature is above 40, the roads are clear, and you can get extra innings and drive your precious rust-prone vintage metal (which always makes you feel like you're cheating death, or fate, or both), or you can get hammered weekly by serial snowstorms that freeze the garage door and literally bury cars in your driveway. Because of this, it really behooves us who live in these climes to think through the winter storage issue. I need to know which cars I'm going to be working on over the winter and thus need to be at the house, and which have reached a plateau of project stability and thus can be shuttled to one of the outlying storage areas. I loved having Bertha at the house, but in early Decemer 2018, I aimed her at Fitchburg, gave her one last glorious thrashing on the drive out, and closed the garage door on her for the season.

Figure 128: Bertha nestled away beneath a leaky roof in Fitchburg in December 2018.

And that brings us to the more complicated question.

The Fate of Bertha

I am not a collector. I'm just a guy who follows his passions, buys and drives what blows his skirt up, tries to keep them all running, and tries to remember to enjoy my cars. That enjoyment comes in a variety of ways. The most dramatic vector for enjoyment is taking the cars on road trips of thousands of miles to events with other like-minded head cases. And, sure, I enjoy hopping in the cars and taking afternoon or evening drives on scenic twisty roads, or to an occasional low-load event like a Cars and Coffee or the wonderful lawn events they have at the Larz Anderson Museum in Brookline. But one of the main ways I enjoy my cars is to have them at the house so I can be able to hop into one of them and run out to pick up a gallon of milk at Trader Joe's on a Sunday morning. It's the automotive equivalent of smiling across the breakfast table at your spouse. Not everything is mind-bending back-arching nail-clawing sex in a Paris hotel room with a view of the Eiffel Tower, nor does it need to be.

Occasionally I will buy something that I think I can make a little money on, but I'm not a dealer or a flipper. I don't buy cars that I don't crave, and money-wise, I'm wrong as often as I'm right. I might make a little money on one car only to lose my shirt on the next. If I was a collector, or looking to make money, I'd be buying the best cars in the best possible condition, as those are the ones that appreciate the most in value. Instead, I do the opposite. I'm a bottom-feeder. But there's a reason for that: I typically buy needy cars because the business model, if you want to call it that, is having satisfying projects that I can write about as I work on them. I joke that I'm the only person I know whose job it is to buy stupid cars I shouldn't buy, resurrect them, and take them on stupid road trips I shouldn't embark on, but it's perilously close to the truth. What would I have to write about if I spent shit tons of money and bought perfect cars? How much money I made when I sold them? Gag me with a giubo.

I've owned my 3.0CSi since 1986. That's the car that'll still be here when the creditors are foreclosing on the house. But the others come and go. I don't subscribe to the whole "custodian" thing that the cars are only passing through us, that they belong to history like the Ark in the first Indiana Jones movie, that we have a responsibility to care for them properly. Feh. While they're here, they're mine, and I'll make whatever decisions I want regarding originality versus modification while I own them, thank you very much. Hell, I'd paint flames on a BMW if I wanted to, and the fact that it'd make certain purists gasp would only add to the appeal. While I do appreciate the passion of people who talk about preserving cars "for the ages," they have income and resources that I don't that allow them to operate at a level that's simply not available to me. Good? Good.

However, I do sometimes think of myself as a foster parent. Cars may sojourn with me for a number of months or years. Sometimes I feel like it's a privilege to have a role in their life, to care for them, to nurse them back to health, to keep the little rascals fed, clothed, legal, happy, and out of trouble, to do the automotive equivalent of getting them in their jammies and reading them a bedtime story until I pass them on to another owner.

Louie and Bertha, as a pair, sort of mark the three-sigma boundaries of a 2002-related bell curve. The sort-out and resurrection of Louie was a book-worthy story, but in addition to that, the car was a remarkably intact original '72 tii, the most valuable 2002 variant sold in the United States through the dealer network. So, yes, it's a car with a great story and a lot of heart, and I love both of those things, and buying it, resurrecting it, and road-tripping it home was one of the most satisfying automotive things I've ever done, but when I bought it (which was, in fact, just after I lost my job), make no mistake, I was keenly aware that it was a smokin' good deal and an excellent investment. The car has appreciated in value since I bought it, and is likely to continue to do so. While that's not why I did it, it made the doing a bit less wacko. One might even think that the purchase was downright rational, and that writing the book was a strategic attempt to boost the car's value. (To be clear, neither of these things are true. The purchase was a crime of opportunity, as most of my purchases are. The swoop-in-and-fix-it-where-it-sits adventure was one I'd long wanted to go on, and the book allowed a great story to be told.)

Bertha stands in stark contrast to Louie. It's got so many strikes against it that, value-wise, it strikes out before it comes to the plate. Even if they're in very good shape, square tail light 2002s don't have the value of the earlier round tail light cars. Plus, it's not a tii. And it's a '75, which is widely viewed as the worst year for 2002s. And far more important than any of that, the car has been, how to say… Bertha'd. I mean, patina is hot right now in the car world, but Bertha's dinner-plate-sized rust blisters and primer-colored door are way beyond patina. And it's still got that hand-sized hole in the driver's side floor and rust ranging from surface oxidation to bubbles to perforations in many other places. The 10:1 pistons, 300 degree cam, Webers, 5-speed, Koni suspension, and other 1980s period-correct mods are of value to me and make it a hoot to drive, but most people can't see past the car's exterior. I said in the "Adding Up The Costs" chapter that I'm thrilled with the $4500-ish it cost me to purchase and resurrect the car, but if I had to sell it, I'd be stunned if I could recoup that. And that's fine. You don't buy a car like Bertha to make money on it. As I'm sure is abundantly clear, I'm attracted not only to a physical car but to the *story* of a car, and story-wise, it doesn't get much better than Bertha.

But, in an environment where only the 3.0CSi is sacred and no other car stays around forever, what is the likely fate of Bertha?

Short to mid-term, I don't see her leaving the Siegel stable anytime soon. As long as I have moderately-priced storage in Fitchburg or elsewhere, there will continue to be a space for her. As I described, my re-purchase of the car was due to an odd confluence of events, but I never could've predicted that the oh-my-god-this-thing-is-just-such-a-hot-rod-hoot-to-drive factor would've been even more significant than the my-wife-and-I-drove-off-from-our-wedding-in-it factor. Having gone through the resurrection and now genuinely enjoying owning and driving the car so much, I can't see why I'd shepherd it on to another owner. (Unless Alex comes crying to my doorstep wanting it back. Actually, he's made me promise to give him first right of refusal if I ever need to sell her.)

So Bertha stays.

But the larger question is how she'll be used. With her heavy patina, rust, and generally beat-up condition, many folks either assume that a) I'll "restore" her (which I put in quotes because anyone asking that question has no idea what it means), or that b) don't really care what happens to her, that I'll daily-drive her in any weather and leave her parked outside. The first, as I said earlier, will never happen, and the second is way far from the truth.

Bertha got her signature rust blisters because the car was carelessly stored in a garage that backed onto a pond, had batts of insulation resting on the hood, and the fiberglass provided a vector for moisture off the pond to corrode the hood, but make no mistake about it, careless storage is way better than no storage. The car is only as solid as it is because it was stored and not left to the mercy of the elements. To take a car that you drove off from your wedding in, that survived 26 years of storage, that you bought back because you have history with it, that you resurrected, and then just run it into the ground through five parts benign carelessness, two parts active neglect, and one part maliciousness, seems all kinds of wrong to me. It'd be like doing what John Malkovich did to Michelle Pfeiffer in *Dangerous Liasons*. I don't do things like that. I am faithful to the people and things I love. At least I try to be.

Patina like Bertha's creates a problem. Expose those rust blisters to too much moisture by leaving the car outside or driving it in the rain too often, and before you know it, the spots will explode into actual holes. I've had folks tell me that I should clear-coat the car to preserve the rust and other patina, but I looked into it, and it's far from a slam-dunk. I don't believe that you can simply spray clear coat on a surface that's not prepared to accept it. Some level of surface sanding would almost certainly be necessary, which means pulling trim off. And flaky rust would almost certainly need to be sanded down to get the sealing product to adhere. That would alter Bertha's appearance. I've read on forums where people report that quick-and-dirty attempts to seal a patina'd finish result in the clear coat darkening from UV exposure, then flaking off. When you see a more-professional treatment where a shop has intentionally distressed and then sealed a finish to give a car a rat-rod look, you're typically looking at a paint job that cost thousands of dollars. It just happens that it's a paint job whose goal it is to produce a distressed finish, not a pretty shiny one.

And more to the point, the blisters on the hood are the most visible of Bertha's rust, but they are, to use the cliché, just the tip of the iceberg. Although I consider the car to be fairly solid, the more you look, the more rust you see. Yes, there's the cereal-bowl-sized hole in the floor behind the pedal bucket, but there's a lot more. There is rust blistering on the right front fender that is transitioning into a rust hole. There's some softness on one rocker. There are areas on the nose and fenders where rust is forming around the flaking paint caused by small dents. There are rust pinholes at the bottom of one door. There is rust on the rear edges of the sunroof. There's surface rust on some areas of the floorboards that in certain areas, like near the rear subframe mounts and the big plugs in the floor pans, is becoming more serious. Where it's on flat accessible areas, I could try and chase it with a grinder and spray it with rust inhibitor and primer, but it's also gotten into inaccessible areas like door, hood, and trunk seams, and the crevices up under the fenders. You can use non-hardening corrosion-inhibiting products like Waxoyl, or Kano Weatherpruf, or even just motor oil. I *do*, in fact, use these sorts of products on my cars, typically brushing or spraying them on any exposed surface rust on a car's undercarriage prior to a road trip. It's better than nothing.

In automotive circles, rust is often referred to as "cancer." It's a fairly apt analogy. Like cancer, isolated non-invasive rust that hasn't spread can be cured, but more often, it has spread, and it takes extraordinary and expensive efforts to send it into remission, after which it will likely come back again and again. On a car like Bertha, basically solid but with rust forming everywhere, its long-term fate is already known: Rust will kill it, and will do so quickly if the car sees consistent moisture. That's the way it is. She's a Dead Bertha Walking. There's no economic scenario that will ever justify full-on restoration. The $20,000 number I floated earlier was what you're quoted these days for a high-quality bare-metal glass-out paint job on a car. To do a full rotisserie restoration and sandblast every crevice is probably three times that.

Let's say that I *was* wealthy enough to foot a $60,000 restoration bill on Bertha… to do *what* with her? Put her back like she was in 1975? Who the hell would want *that*? It's not even clear what I would turn the car into if I *wanted* to throw ridiculous sums of money at it. The car's whole appeal is its story and its Keith-Richards-like "yeah, bitches, I'm still here" stubbornness, and the poignant and ephemeral nature of the use of an object whose lifetime is obviously finite. Just like us. Maire Anne knows, if the *Overhaulin'* producers ever come knocking, to slam the door in their fucking faces.

In 2011, I wrote a piece for *Roundel* magazine called "The Lion in Winter," trading on the classic film of the same name with Peter O'Toole and Katherine Hepburn about an English king who's past his prime. The piece was about a shabby Euro M635CSi I saw advertised in upsate New York. The ad sounded appealing enough that I drove out there with cash and a trailer, but when I arrived, I found that the car had fist-sized rust holes in the fenders, and needed, well, everything. Although the car was still quite fast, and made great M88 engine noises, its condition was so bad that it was teetering on the edge of being a running parts car.

Whether a given amount of rust is a death sentence is, of course, relative to a car's market value. If "the lion" was instead an E-Type Jaguar or a '63 split-windowed Corvette or a long-hood 911, you'd brag to all your friends what an easy restoration you just scored. And with the appreciating value of M6s and M635CSis, it may be that, over the past eight years, the lion crossed the line to being worth restoring. But I doubt it.

Even though I walked away from it, I found it hard to let the idea of the lion go. Here's what I wrote: "Maybe I could give the car a few extra innings. I could replace the one grossly perforated fender, weld up the exhaust, fix the front end, soak the underside in Waxoyl, and smile every time I stand on it and hear the howl of the Bavarian Ferrari's twin cams. I could send it off, loved. I find myself oddly preoccupied with the lion, hoping that circumstances deliver him to my door. I may not be able to nurse him back to his former health, but a part of me hopes he can live out his days on my preserve, maybe kill and eat a few squirrels in my backyard."

I think about that because the words apply eerily well to Bertha. There's the poignant part: "I could send it off, loved." But there's also a terribly practical part: "He could live out his days on my preserve." Usually we think about buying cars to fit a certain set of circumstances. If it's a daily driver, we're looking for a car to commute in and drive the family around, which requires some balance of passenger room, cargo capacity, terrain handling, power, fuel economy, reliability, cost, etc. If it's a collector car, we're looking to satisfy parameters of cost and condition, and then show and store the car. But instead, with Bertha, as it was with the lion, this dynamic was flipped around to *looking for a set of circumstances that will fit the car.* It's like an elderly person who can no longer garden but still enjoys tending the flowers in the window box.

The other extreme is, ironically, treating Bertha like it's a pretty shiny hangar queen—religiously keeping it out of the moisture *because* of its distressed finish. That also feels unnatural to me.

Those are the endpoints of the usage envelope, goalposts through which I need to kick the use of the car—neither being afraid to use it, nor saying "fuck it it's already destroyed I don't care what happens to it."

Because of Bertha's long storage prior to resurrection, I can't help but think of Jessie, the cowgirl from *Toy Story 2*. I imagine Bertha, like Jessie, having felt loved by her owner (me, then Alex), then abandoned during her 26 years of storage, then overjoyed at her rescue, and now anxious at the thought of being put back into storage. So I am sensitive to the possibility that what's in store for her is that, after being resurrected and showered with attention and love, she'll just become one of eight lightly-used vintage cars. Is she going to be like the prospector Stinky Pete? No. He was "mint in the box." Bad analogy. Scratch that. Really, she should be more like Woody—a toy that's played with, even if that means getting his arm ripped off and having a kid replace it with a ridiculously overstuffed one.

So I hatched a plan.

Vintage Prep

To consummate our reconnection, Bertha and I clearly needed a road trip. Better still, a *couple* of road trips. Fortunately, the vintage BMW world is rife with such opportunities. The plan was to first take Bertha the 3,000 miles to and from MidAmerica 02Fest, held annually in Eureka Springs Arkansas at the end of April. (I'd driven Kugel to MidAmerica in 2015 and had a great time.) Then, in May, I'd bring Bertha to The Vintage in Asheville, an event I've attended since 2010. Together, the 5,000 miles to and from these two informal and welcoming events would collectively constitute a great big coming-out party for Bertha and let her strut her stuff in a fun and non-judgmental environment without other cars going mean girl on her and Bertha pulling a *Carrie*. Not that I've seen Bertha go psycho on anyone, but look at her. She could totally do that shit.

Several things intervened. The first was the Lotus, that pretty little British interloper that had been sitting dead in the corner of the garage for nearly six years since I bought it in June of 2013 as a present to myself when my first book was published. You can see the car covered in boxes and surrounded by crap in many of the previous photographs, and the freshly-resurrected car in the photo below. The Lotus will likely be the subject of another book, but long story short, the reassembly of its engine was awaiting the arrival of a long-out-of-stock custom water pump and front timing cover, and in the kind of thing you can't make up, they arrived in the mail literally on Christmas Eve 2018. I decided, Scarlett O'Hara-style that, as god is my witness, this *would* be the winter of the Lotus. (It was also the winter of my discontent, but that's another story). With a focus and a drive that's unusual even for me, during the first four months of 2019, I got the Lotus' engine rebuilt, mated to the transaxle, the drivetrain back in the car, and the car running and capable of moving under its own power. That was great, but obviously, while I was laser-focused on the Lotus, I wasn't working on Bertha; she was still sitting out in Fitchburg.

Figure 129: In the spring of 2019, Bertha did have some pretty stiff competition for my attention.

Figure 130: The British interloper and Bertha come nose to nose.

Second, I had prostate cancer. It was the good kind with all the good words—contained, non-invasive, low-grade, low-volume—and was treated with brachytherapy, which is implantation of little radioactive seeds. One outpatient procedure, done, cured. As cancer goes, pretty easy. (Well, other than being sent home with a catheter the size of a spark plug wire going into my dick and having to live with it for a week, but that's another story.) But, as with anything with radiation, it *did* leave me with bouts of fatigue that had not completely abated by the time driving season hit. And, as anything with the prostate goes, it *did* change my peeing. I used to think nothing of jumping in a car and pounding out 800 miles in a day. If anything, sitting on my old swollen prostate while driving made it so I had to urinate *less* often. After the procedure, though, even when I was working in the garage, I found that the step from "I need to pee" to "I need to pee RIGHT NOW" was sharper and more rapid than it used to be. As the big season clock swung around to spring and my focus finally began turning to Bertha, I wondered whether jumping in the car and banging out the two 750-mile days needed to get to MidAmerica 02Fest was simply too much too soon.

I was right on the line, trying to decide whether MidAmerica was feasible, when the third hiccup occurred. My remarkable 89-year-old mother's health began to fail. The doctors first thought she was experiencing a recurrence of the pneumonia she'd had in the fall, but it turned out to be more serious than that, though we didn't know that at the time. She spent eight harrowing days in the hospital. She appeared to recover, at least temporarily, but obviously everything got put on hold. The timing was such that I thought "Thank *god* I am not on my way to Arkansas."

For all three of these reasons, it wasn't until the beginning of May 2019 that I even got out to Fitchburg to wake Bertha up from her winter slumber, assure her I hadn't abandoned her, and bring her back to Newton. With me largely recovered, and with my mother's health apparently stable, I began planning the trip to The Vintage in mid-May.

During the drive back home, I had a punch list of leftover issues in my head, but cars feel the way they feel, exuding whatever vibe they have. Bertha's vibe wasn't "I'm not ready for this; I've still got some issues." Instead it clearly was "You fool, I want to *run!*" Fortunately, there really wasn't that much.

I began the work by examining my own list of the "The Big Seven." I've written about this quite a bit in my online pieces for Hagerty and BimmerLife, and also cover it in *Ran When Parked*. The idea here is that while anything *can* break on a vintage car, most often it *doesn't*, and instead the things that are most likely to strand a vintage car fall into one of the following seven categories:

Ignition: Bertha was still running around on the points and condenser that were in her when I woke her from her 26-year snooze. This may seem like folly, but the quality of new points and condensers, even OEM ones, has gone to shit. Much has been written about points that have the nylon separation block snap off and condensers that fail within five miles, so using old but proven ignition parts actually makes more sense than you'd think. But that didn't mean I wanted to leave it that way for a nearly 2000-mile round-trip drive. There's an active debate about the whole points versus Pertronix thing (indeed, I got more comments about an article I wrote for Hagerty about it than anything else I ever did for them), but, for long trips, I come down firmly on the side of Pertronix or other electronic triggering, as you don't need to worry about the condenser frying or your points closing up on the Tappan Zee Bridge.

For a 2002, the most commonly-used electronic triggering module is from Pertronix. I've had them in many cars, and the only failures I've had is when I've wired them wrong. They cost about $85. However, I found a vendor on eBay selling a similar module from Hotspark for $40. I searched on bmw2002faq.com for reviews, and was delighted that the gestalt seemed to be "basically the same as a Pertronix, basically as reliable." I installed and tested it, and was delighted by the fact that the rubber grommet that goes out the condenser hole was easier to install than the one for the Pertronix.

Figure 131: The Hotspark ignition module installed in Bertha. Yes, I added some slack to that black wire.

After swapping the points for the Hotspark, the timing needed to be reset. Usually the way I do this is to set it by the book, then advance it until, under load and one gear higher than you'd usually use (like 5th gear going up a hill at 60mph), it pings just slightly, but never pings during normal load. However, knowing that the route to The Vintage in Asheville includes a spectacular section that runs through the mountains with long uphill grades, and knowing that Bertha's balky transmission prevents easy 5th to 4th downshifts, I left the timing retarded by about two degrees further than where I'd normally set it so it wouldn't knock at all, even under extreme load conditions.

Fuel Delivery: Bertha has a highly non-stock fuel delivery system consisting of a pair of Weber 40DCOE sidedraft carbs fed by a trunk-mounted electric fuel pump, all installed in the mid-1980s. When I resurrected the car, I found that the metal fuel line running under the car had rusted and was leaking near the front. At the time, I cut off the rusted section and ran a longer length of rubber fuel hose to it. So, fuel-prep-wise, the first thing I needed to do was inspect the rest of the metal line. To my dismay, I discovered that other sections of the metal line had the unmistakable "coffee cake" look of non-trivial corrosion you often see on brake lines before they burst. In addition, I found that, contrary to my memory, I had *not* replaced all of the rubber fuel hose under the car; the long section that leads from the tank to the back end of the metal line was clearly decades old. And the fact that the electric fuel pump itself had been installed during the heyday of MTV gave me pause.

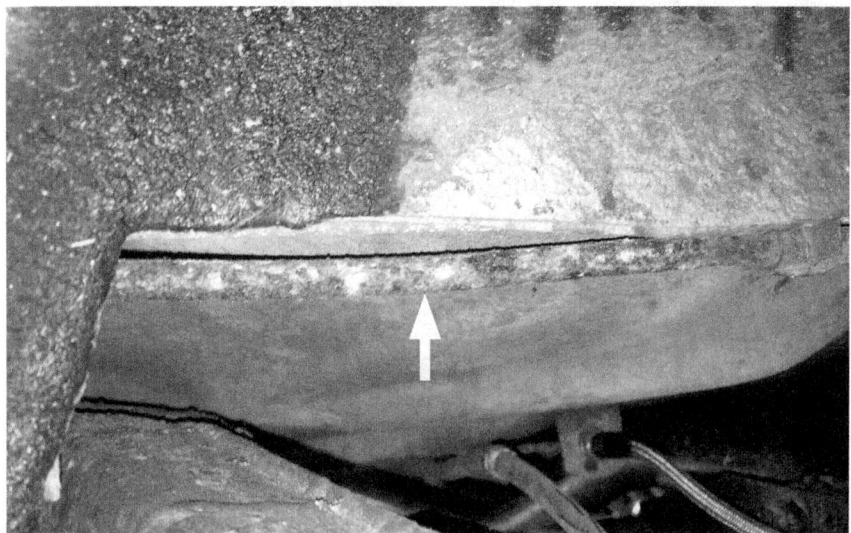

Figure 132: A worrisome section of "coffee cake" rust on the metal fuel line.

I addressed all three issues. On a stock '75 2002, the metal line is actually the fuel return line; it's the white plastic line that runs inside the car that's the fuel send line. When I built Bertha, I originally planned it to be a fuel-injected tii tribute car, and in a tii, since the fuel pressure is much higher than in a carbureted 2002, the metal line *is* the fuel send line, so I plumbed it that way, but then wound up using the Webers instead. To set it right and tight, I blew out the long-unused white plastic line with compressed air, and plumbed the fuel system using it instead of the metal line as a carbureted 2002 usually does. I'd bought a little EMPI electric fuel pump for the Lotus, but then wound up repairing that car's mechanical fuel pump, which left the electric pump up for grabs. I used it to replace Bertha's 34-year-old electric pump, mounting it lower in Bertha's trunk and with a less circuitous route than the previous pump. I then connected everything using new fuel hose and band clamps. Done.

Figure 133: The new fuel pump was relocated and plumbed in a less circuitous manner.

Shortly after this, my friend Lindsey Brown mentioned to me that he'd prophylactically replaced the aging electric fuel pump in his 2002, only to have the new one fail, requiring him to reinstall the original one on the side of the road. I take omens like this seriously and thought about swapping them back, but left the new pump in place and brought the old one as a spare.

Cooling System: This one was a tough choice. I'd installed a factory tropical radiator in Bertha in the 1980s, so at least the radiator was 34 years old, not 44. When I resurrected the car, I drained the cooling system, wasn't horrified at what came out, rocked the fins on the water pump fan fore-and-aft to check for play in the pump bearing, thought it was fine, scraped the corrosion off the aluminum coolant necks, and replaced any hoses that were either pillow-y soft or rock hard. On the one hand, I've made a career out of preaching prophylactic maintenance of the cooling system, and you never know what corroded horror will greet you until you remove the water pump, but I'd driven the car during hot weather, and cooling-wise, things seemed absolutely fine. If anything, it ran *too* cool, rarely getting above 1/3 of the way up the temperature gauge. I decided to leave it alone and traveled with a spare water pump. I also threw an unused Spectra metal 320i radiator in the trunk. Of course, when you don't trust your cooling system enough to be traveling with a water pump *and* a spare radiator, you need to ask yourself if you're making the right decision.

Charging System: I'd already installed a new internally-regulated alternator and an extra grounding strap to the engine.

Belts: The water pump-alternator belt had already been replaced, though I always bring a spare anyway. And the new alternator has new bushings, so there's no issue of worn alternator bushings causing the belt to loosen. The a/c belt was also new.

Clutch Hydraulics: I'd already replaced both the master and slave cylinders.

Ball Joints: These seem like an artificial addition to my list of the "Big Seven," but ball joints sit at the nexus of the steering and the suspension, they take all the pounding from bumps and potholes, and if they fail catastrophically, the wheel folds under the fender well like a broken ankle, and you lose control of the car. The ball joints in 2002s are originally riveted to the lower control arms, so if you find ones with the rivets still there, they've been in there since Nixon or Ford were in office. 02 ball joints are usually quite sturdy, but if the rubber boots tear, moisture and dirt can get it in and ruin them. Bertha is running on her original ball joints, but the boots looked fine, and they passed the "squeeze 'em with a big pair of channel lock pliers to look for play" test.

Figure 134: Bertha's original riveted ball joints didn't appear to have any play.

While I was checking out the front end, though, I did notice that the left front wheel bearing was a little loose. I removed the cotter pin, tightened the castellated nut by one notch, verified that, as per the manual, I could still move the big washer with a screwdriver, and re-pinned it.

With "The Big Seven" addressed (or, in the case of the cooling system, ignored at my own peril), I then addressed the following Bertha-specific issues.

Valve Adjustment and Oil Change: These are things you should do shortly after an engine has had work as well as before a long trip. Bertha's head was rebuilt the previous summer, so both of these steps were overdue.

Driveshaft Alignment: As I wrote earlier, driveshaft alignment is critical to a successful 5-speed conversion. Ironically, the giubo, or flex disc, doesn't really like to flex. It's not a universal joint. It's now accepted practice that, if necessary, the center support bearing be shimmed lower, or transmission be shimmed either down or up to improve the alignment. However, when I installed Bertha's 5-speed 34 years ago, this kind of attention was rarely paid. During the car's resurrection, after I replaced the cracked giubo, I found that the new one was obviously distorted, and tried to address the issue by using washers to lower the center support bearing by an almost comical amount. This made alignment slight better, but clearly something was still amiss.

Figure 135: Bertha's giubo was clearly distorted.

If you're using a U-shaped transmission support bracket as many 5-speed installations do, you can monkey with the alignment by shimming the transmission up (putting washers under the support bushing) or down (putting washers under the bracket), but Bertha has an ultra-rare Metric Mechanic transmission support bracket that doesn't allow for any upward adjustment. Further, the yawning rust hole behind Bertha's pedal bucket comes jarringly close to the left-hand transmission mounting tab, so the idea of putting a ratchet wrench on the bolt on that tab and applying any torque to it gave me the willies.

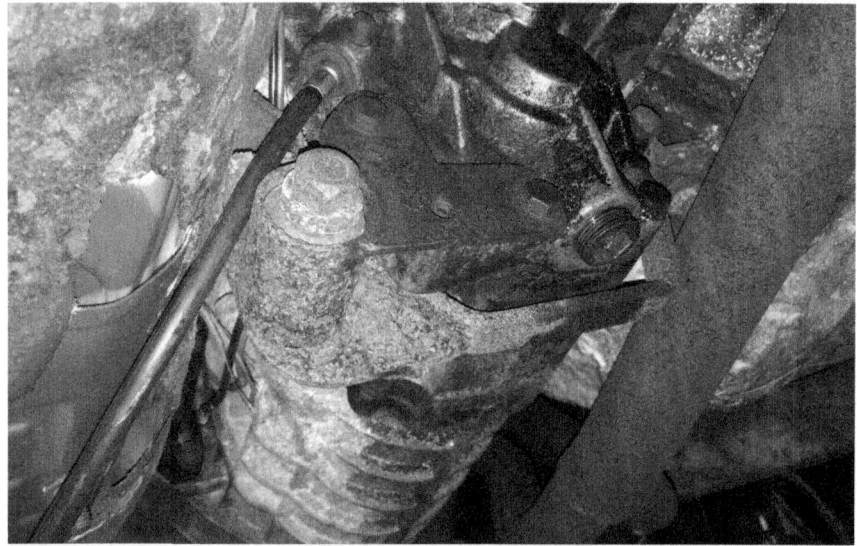

Figure 136: This shows Bertha's unusual Metric Mechanic transmission mount, and the alarming proximity of the left transmission mounting tab to the rust hole behind the pedal bucket.

I thought that I had a traditional U-shaped transmission support bracket that I could try, but I tore apart the garage and could not find it. In the end, I loosened the giubo, removed the washers, re-did the "gap test," determined that I'd gotten the shimming correct (or as correct as it could be) during the car's resurrection, put everything back together the way it was and made a note to bring a spare giubo for the trip in case this one self-destructed.

As I said earlier, Bertha's 5-speed transmission has a horrible 4th gear synchro, so in my mind, I roll that and the driveshaft alignment issues together. Some winter, when I have a lot of time on my hands, I'll pull the trani, remove the pedal bucket, fix the floor, maybe install the 5-speed of unknown condition that's been sitting under my back porch for ten years, and align things properly. It's a nice fantasy. Yeah, this will never get done.

Door Locks: Neither of Bertha's doors would lock. The ignition key wouldn't turn in either door handle, and neither push button would go down, so I couldn't even do the reach-over thing. That's not a big deal for a lightly-used around-town car, but it did have two impacts on a car I was about to road trip to The Vintage. The first was that I'd need to pull my valuables out when I stopped for fuel and ran into the rest room. The second was that, as you'll read in "The Wegweiserization" chapter, my friend Paul Wegweiser has a tradition of pranking me and my cars at The Vintage, and without being able to lock the doors, there was zero chance of keeping Paul out of my car.

I pulled off both door cards, lubricated the locking plates, and got the push-buttons to work. Next, I removed the door handles and lubricated the tumblers, but the problem seemed to be that the key didn't match. Bertha had twice been stolen while Alex had her, and while neither Alex nor I recalled re-keying the ignition, anything was possible.

Then I remembered that I had recently gotten a free faux tii. Well, it wasn't as if I'd actually *forgotten* about it. It was sitting ten feet away in my driveway with "parts car" written all over it. I pulled the key from its ignition, tried it in both of its door locks, and marveled at my good fortune that both worked. So I pulled the door handles from the faux tii, swapped them with Bertha's handles, and put the faux tii's key on Bertha's ring.

Figure 137: Nothing like having a parts car in your driveway with working keyed door locks just when you need them.

Before I buttoned up the door cards, I re-grommeted the lock rods in the driver's door. I'd done this in the passenger door when I replaced the smashed window, but the grommets were all missing in the driver's door, which caused it to rattle like a bunch of coat hangers fucking on rusty bedsprings in a motel on the seedy side of town.

Figure 138: Missing grommets in the locking mechanism create door rattles that can drive you nuts.

Snapped Rear Wheel Stud: When I first pulled the wheels off Bertha in Alex's neighbor's garage to un-seize the drums, one of the studs on the left rear wheel snapped. I'd been comfortable driving around locally on three lug nuts, but 2000 miles at highway speeds was another matter. Experience has shown me that you only have a few seconds from "What's that metallic rumble? Could the lug nuts be loose?" to the wheel flying off at speed.

I read up on bmw2002faq.com on replacing a broken stud. While there is enough room to drive the stud out with the hub still on the spindle, it's not really advised; if you really wail on it with a sledge, you can bend the hub or spindle or damage the bearing. I tried heating up the stud with the oxy-acetylene torch and giving it a love tap, but it didn't budge. So I tried to pull the hub. I got the big castellated nut off, but could not pull the hub off the spindle despite using heat. I went back to Plan A. I cut the broken stud off flush with the flange, heated it up cherry red with the torch, and using a hammer and a punch, popped it out with minimal effort. Should've done that the first time. I hoped I didn't damage anything trying to heat and pull the hub.

Figure 139: The old "heat and beat" worked perfectly removing the snapped stud.

Install Cibié Oscars

As I described earlier, during my original ownership of Bertha, she proudly wore a set of Cibié Oscar driving lights on her massive bridge abutment of a front bumper. When I rescued her from the garage where she'd been sitting for 26 years, only the Cibié's housings were present. I later found the lenses under the seats, but the lighting elements were trashed. At the time, I put the non-functional lenses back in to retain the look. But then, when I did the bumper conversion, the Cibiés were lost, and with them, part of Bertha's swagger. Though I liked the small bumpers, I felt like I'd taken part of Bertha's personality away, like a facelift she didn't want.

Figure 140: Bertha before and after the facelift.

Then, my friend Alan Hunter Johansson conspired with Maire Anne to send her a mint set of Cibiés he'd had on his Volvo 122. I promised to install them when the dust had settled on the car's resurrection. Then the bumper swap happened, I needed to drill holes to install them, yadda yadda. They'd been sitting on a shelf in the garage since then.

As I was clocking through the punch list to get down to The Vintage, I came to the line that said "install Cibiés." My left brain thought "No, they're not important." My right brain overruled it and said "Yes, they are."

Initially I thought I'd just mount them for show, but Bertha has the factory fog light switch to the left of the instrument cluster, and it beckoned to be hooked up. And, having written an electrical book, I now know how to wire them properly, with the fog light switch tripping a relay, and the Cibiés wired to it with beefy 12-gauge wire. (The old ones were literally spliced into the high beam wires on the back of the headlights with wire nuts and thin speaker wire. It's a wonder I didn't burn the car down.)

I hoped that I didn't have much, if any, night driving on this trip, but I was now prepared to stun deer at the length of a football field if I did. And, more importantly, Bertha's got that "Hello, boys" face again. Thanks Alan!

Figure 141: Bertha with her Cibié-fueled candlepower blazing.

Speaking of lighting, two days before leaving for The Vintage, I was using an evening ice cream run as an excuse for a shakedown cruise. At a traffic light, a guy pulled up next to me and motioned me to roll the window down. This happens a lot while driving any vintage BMW, perhaps more so in Bertha due to her, uh, striking appearance. But to my surprise, the fellow said "Hey buddy, do you know that all your rear lights are out?" I pulled over, and sure enough, only the license plate lights were on.

It was very likely that it was a grounding issue, so when I got home, I searched for the ground location in the trunk, but couldn't find it. I looked on bmw2002faq.com (which is still the most complete repository of most 2002-related information on the planet) and found a post that described the ground point near driver's side tail light. I searched for it, and there it was. And the nut on it was loose. I took it off, cleaned the ring terminals, and bingo, that fixed everything except the right brake light which turned out to have a spade connector that had popped out the back of its plastic socket.

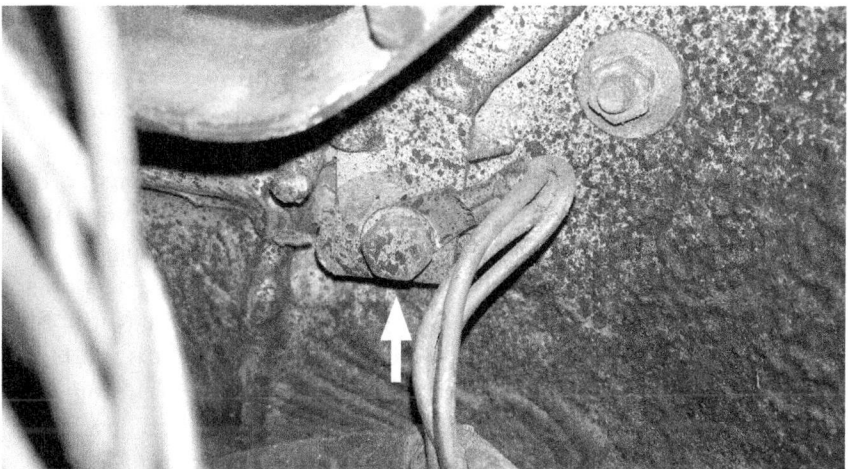

Figure 142: The trunk ground connection I couldn't find.

Wheels

As I've said, I really wanted silver E30 steel wheels for Bertha, as that's what I almost put on her in the 1980s, but I never found a set. After her resurrection, Bertha was running around on silver E30 basketweave alloys given to me by Bob Sawtelle, but as I was preparing to leave for The Vintage, they weren't on the car. The reason why was that, at some point in late fall, I thought that I might sell Kugel. For years, Kugel had worn a set of gold E30 basketweaves. These are rare wheels, as they were only available on, I believe, '91 and '92 E30 convertibles. I originally had them on an Agave (green) '02, on which I thought they looked great. But I was never completely sold on their look against Kugel's white paint, and I was concerned that potential buyers might feel the same. So in December 2018, before I put Bertha away for the season, I temporarily swapped wheels, putting the silver E30 'weaves on Kugel and the gold ones on Bertha. The silver ones looked less controversial on Kugel (which was the idea), but I absolutely loathed the way the gold ones looked on Bertha. After all, part of Bertha's appeal to me were the period-correct '80s mods, and these particular gold E30 'weaves never would've been on a 2002 in the 1980s. Many of my Facebook friend, however, thought that the gold wheels added snap to Bertha's appearance. I suppose they did, but it made the car veer uncomfortably close to hooptie, which was the antithesis of the look I wanted. So, before her big coming out party at The Vintage, I wanted to swap the wheels back.

However, as I was about to pull the car out of the garage in Fitchburg, I thought out loud to myself, "You haven't seen Bertha in five months. Keep an open mind about the wheels." I drove it out, parked it on the street, looked at it, and thought… "Actually, I don't hate it." So the gold basketweaves stayed for the trip.

But the decision to leave them on triggered a poignant memory. In the early 1990s, when my car guy friend Dave Gelineau was dying, I went to see him. Dave was always a man of very strong opinions, and a little thing like dying certainly wasn't going to change that. To no one's surprise, we started talking about cars. Dave lit into the Mitsubishi GT3000 VR4, which, for reasons unclear, raised his particular ire. His cancer-stricken haze lifted, and he became quite animated, hurling venom and invective against Japanese "posers." I calmed him down, saying things like "different strokes," "no accounting for taste," etc. "Yeah," I guess so," Dave said, with a sense of forced accommodation. Then, the rage turned back on. "*Except,*" he said, "for those people who put gold mesh wheels on German cars. Whenever I see those on a Porsche or a BMW, you can *not* tell me that that guy is not a fuckin' asshole." For that reason alone, those gold E30 basketweaves can *not* stay on Bertha for the long term.

Figure 143: Kugel and Bertha wearing their swapped shoes.

All totaled, Bertha's vintage prep was going swimmingly.

Right up until I saw...

The Cracked Subframe

The front subframe on 2002s have an ear that stands vertically to support the left-hand engine mount. With age and pounding, it's very common for this ear to crack part-way up. This happened on Kugel a few years ago. After I'd loaned it to Jeremy and Corinne to drive off from their wedding in, I heard a lot of metallic rumbling, and found that Kugel's engine was badly cocked to the left. When I crawled under and examined the ear on the subframe, I found that it had cracked, and the upper half had slid down over the lower half. To fix it in Kugel, I held the engine up using a ratchet strap and a 2×4, dropped the front subframe out of the car, and took it to my friend Tom Samuelson who welded the crack and braced it with additional metal. I then reinstalled the subframe. The entire endeavor was as much work as it sounds like it is.

Figure 144: The engine mounting ear on Kugel's front subframe, shown during the welding repair.

What I found on Bertha wasn't anything like that. It wasn't a fully-separated crack like Kugel had, but instead an un-separated fracture. And, reassuringly, there was no fresh clean metal showing. It was likely that the crack had formed decades ago.

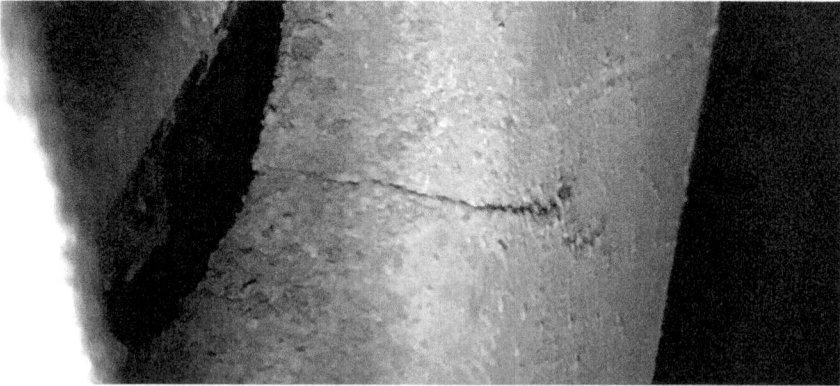

Figure 145: Fortunately, the crack in Bertha's front subframe had not separated.

I could've done several things. Since I now own a welder, I could've dropped the subframe and tried to weld it myself. I could've taken it to my friend Tom. I could've inspected the faux tii parts car in my driveway and, if its subframe was un-cracked, swapped it in.

Instead, I did none of these things. Since the crack looked like it hadn't grown in quite some time, I packed a piece of 2×4 and a ratchet strap so that, if the crack broke open, I could, if necessary, lift up the left side of the engine and try to limp the car on down the road that way. Hey, if you're going to be in denial, you might as well go all-in.

Keeping Bertha Cold

There were a few other last-moment sort-out issues. Since I'd fully rebuilt Bertha's air conditioning system, including new hoses and fittings, along with a new parallel flow condenser, I expected to simply turn it on and enjoy cold air in the cabin. Imagine my surprise when, instead, it blew warm. I hooked up the gauges and discovered that the refrigerant had clearly leaked out over winter.

First, I used the UV light and yellow glasses to illuminate the dye in the refrigerant oil and see if I could locate the leak that way, but there was no glowing gun, just small traces left over from the installation. I know that other folks swear by dye, and I use it, but for me it's rarely been the smoking fluorescent gun others experience.

Next, I pumped the system full of nitrogen and just listened. I discovered that it was leaking from the fitting on the input hose to the drier, which, incredibly, wasn't even hand-tight. How it ever held that first summer, who knows. I tightened it, but when I pressure-tested the system again, it still leaked. I chased the leaks with soap solution and found that they were coming from two of my crimp-on hose fittings. I re-crimped them, tested it a third time, and this time it held. After evacuation and recharge (R134a on this car), it was back to blowing cold; the vent temperature probe read 32 degrees. Granted, it wasn't very hot in my garage when I recharged it, but this was reassuring. At a minimum, it restored a shred of credibility and dignity to a guy who wrote an air conditioning book yet apparently botched some aspects of his own a/c installation.

Figure 146: THAT's what you want to see.

The Sunroof Seal

The final prep task was fixing the sunroof seal, which was so deteriorated that, at freeway speeds, the wind had ripped it out of its groove and caused it to mercilessly flog the roof. I'm not a big fan of sunroofs; I've always felt that, if you want the sun on your face, sunroofs are a poor substitute for a convertible. I hadn't opened Bertha's sunroof even once since resurrecting the car. I was about to use the quick-and-dirty approach of caulking the sunroof shut with clear silicone, but then remembered that the widow of a Boston CCA chapter member had given me a pile of parts a couple of years back, and I thought it possible that a sunroof seal might be in the stash. I couldn't believe my good fortune when I found both pieces, undamaged.

I carefully cranked Bertha's sunroof open. It was slightly cocked, but still functional. An hour or so later, I had both pieces installed, and once the glue was dry, I carefully cranked it closed. I may well leave it closed, but even still, the seal is way better than caulk.

Figure 147: The sunroof seal partway through installation. Robby the Robot on the Forbidden Planet poster can now drop Anne Frances in through the sunroof.

With prep complete, I packed Bertha with the usual assortment of tools and parts, and prepared to leave on Wednesday morning. One thing I *didn't* pack was my aluminum floor jack and aluminum jack stands. Why? Because they were still in the trunk of Louie, which had been at the Icon exhibit at the BMW CCA Foundation for a year. I thought about buying another aluminum floor jack and stands, but instead I threw a very small floor jack, suitable for little more than changing a tire, in the trunk. So, for the first time, I didn't pack jack stands for a road trip, figuring that if I really needed jack stands to fix something while on the road, one of my companions could run and buy them.

It was a decision I would come to regret.

The Road Trip

The plan was to travel to The Vintage in Asheville with most of last year's crew—Andrew Wilson, Jose Rosario, Bob Sawtelle, and myself, with Andrew in his E28 M5 and the rest of us in our 2002s. Three other New Englanders contacted us via Facebook and asked to caravan with us.

A few days before departure, Jose reported that the newly-installed engine in his 2002 appeared to have a cracked block. Obviously there were discussions to be had with the person who took ten months to install the engine, but in the meantime, Jose was resigned to taking his E46.

Ironically, after fixing Bertha's a/c, what I really needed on the Wednesday morning departure was heat. The previous night, a freak mini-Nor'Easter had moved into New England. We didn't get snow, but it was about 40 degrees when I left my house. I slid Bertha's heater lever to on, and shivered waiting for warm air to pour through the vents. It never came. When I arrived at the convoy's meeting point, I found that the Bowden cable had broken at the heater valve, requiring me to open the hood and open or close the valve by hand.

We all met at the Charlton service plaza on I-90 at 7am Wednesday morning. I was concerned that six cars were probably too many to stay in formation. That, however, resolved itself in an odd way, and before we left, the caravan suddenly contracted in size. First, Bob Sawtelle bailed. With a pale face, he explained that he had a kidney stone that was in the process of passing, had hoped it would resolve itself before the trip, but now knew he should either drive home or to the hospital. It broke his heart not to go, but he knew that it would be insanity. Andrew and I, who had both been in this situation a few years back (I missed Vintage 2011 for the same reason), reassured him he was making the only choice to be made. I spoke with Bob later in the day and learned that he was okay, but deeply disappointed.

Then the other three fellows—the last-minute additions to the caravan—decided to take a different route, heading west on I-84 instead of snaking down the Merritt Parkway as we were planning to do. We agreed to meet up along the way. So, suddenly we were down to three.

At about 8am, the shrunken caravan of Andrew Wilson in his M5, Jose Rosario in his E46, and me in Bertha bringing down the property values, began the two-day trek from Massachusetts down to Asheville. It's about 900 miles from my house to the host hotel for The Vintage. I've done it in a day, but by the end, I felt like someone had rolled my brain and eyeballs in sand. Two days is better. The first day destination was Staunton, Virginia, which is nearly 2/3 of the way.

All was going well until we reached Allentown, Pennsylvania. Andrew radioed that the oil light in his M5 just came on, and we immediately pulled into the breakdown lane. "Oil pressure, or oil level light?" I asked, imagining catastrophic damage to his expensive S38 engine if it had lost oil pressure. "Oil level," he said. Sure enough, we found that the oil level wasn't even reaching the dipstick. Fortunately, I'd thrown a five-quart jug of Castrol into Bertha's trunk. The M5 drank more than half of it. That oil level warning light probably saved Andrew's S38.

Unfortunately, shortly after we were underway, Jose noticed that, while following the M5, his windshield was getting coated with oil dripping from the car. Right; so the M5 had been low on oil because oil was actively leaking. It should've dawned on us to check that, but for safety reasons, I try to keep intervention on interstate breakdown lanes to as short a time as possible.

We took the next exit and pulled into a parking lot. I donned a Tyvek suit, crawled under the car, and found oil dripping at a pretty good rate from the left side of the block, but I couldn't localize the source. Andrew called Mario Langsten at VSR1 who maintains the M5. Mario said the leak was likely coming from a failed oil pressure switch located behind the alternator and above the power steering pump. From what I was seeing, this made perfect sense. But I've never worked on an S38 engine, and I wasn't sure if you needed to pull the upper radiator hose to remove the alternator. And more to the point, we didn't have the part.

Andrew located a BMW dealership about eight miles away. As long as the oil level was full, the leak didn't seem to be large enough to put the engine at risk for the short drive. Unfortunately, the dealer didn't have the pressure switch in stock (not that we were even certain that that was the problem), and couldn't work on the car until the next day anyway. Andrew offered that Jose and I should continue on without him, but we rejected that outright (our caravanning motto is "safety in numbers, no one left behind"). We discussed other options, such as buying a set of jack stands and fixing it ourselves, but without the part in hand, it was a moot point. Andrew reluctantly decided to leave the M5 at the dealer, ride down with Jose in the E46, and hopefully pick the car up on the way back. Once word was put out on Facebook about what had happened, E28 good guy Aaron Manderbach chimed in that he was only about 30 minutes from Allentown and had the pressure switch, but we were already hundreds of miles south by then. You make the best decisions you can based on the facts that you have at the moment.

Figure 148: Andrew Wilson left his M5 at the dealer and gave me his best "I am so disappointed" face.

Oh. Bertha. This is supposed to a book about Bertha. Where was Bertha during all of this?

Only being a total rock star. The dual Weber 40DCOEs and the 300 degree cam displayed a few flat spots and stumbles at certain RPMs, and 4th gear synchro in the 5-speed was so bad that, to downshift to 4th, I needed to put it into 3rd and *then* 4th, and there were some less-than-smooth wheel and drivetrain resonances at certain speeds, but other than that, the car purred. She seemed blissfully happy to be part of a road trip after all those years in captivity.

Bertha did have one mechanical issue on the drive down that was bad enough for me to stop and intervene. An intermittent snotty-sounding rumble became progressively worse, sounding like a transmission bearing or center support bearing about to let go. I pulled into a rest area to check it out, but I had only the small floor jack and no jack stands. I drove to the end of the rest area and found a little service alcove where I could jack the car on cement instead of asphalt. The area even had a few tree trunks I could put under the frame rails. I crawled under just long enough to see that the source of the noise was nothing more than the exhaust headpipe touching the transmission support bracket. Once I knew that it wasn't a big deal, my brain filtered out the noise instead of imaging that my balky transmission was about to blow up.

Figure 149: This little alcove at a rest area on I-81 seemed tailor-made for Bertha. Note the tree trunks on the left.

We reached Staunton Virginia by about 7 pm on Wednesday evening. That left only about 5 ½ hours of driving on Thursday. As we ran the last section of the drive over the mountains and into Asheville, I was glad I'd left the timing slightly retarded, as the heat appeared to make Bertha's balky 4th gear synchro even worse, making me sometimes leave it in 5th as low as 60 mph and drop it down to 3rd on the big hills. We arrived at the event hotel in Asheville the following day at about 1:30 in the afternoon. I've never had such an early arrival.

Figure 150: Bertha and the boys, triumphant at their arrival at the host hotel for The Vintage.

While Bertha was parked in the hotel parking lot, someone alerted me that the right rear tire appeared to have rub marks on it. Sure enough, due to a combination of the right rear quarter panel being slightly pushed in due to accident damage when the car had been stolen in about 1990, and the amount of weight in the trunk, there was miniscule clearance between the right rear fender lip and the tire. I took a ratchet handle and tried to roll the lip under, but had only marginal success. For the rest of the trip, every time I took a hard left turn, I cringed thinking of the tire rubbing.

By the end of the day on Thursday, Andrew had heard from the dealer that the problem with the M5 was indeed a leaky oil pressure switch, and that the car was all fixed. We planned to pick it up when we went back through Allentown on Monday.

So, after being locked in Alex's neighbor's garage for 26 years, and then rescued and resurrected by yours truly, Bertha was as happy as an indoor cat that's escaped the house. Other than the exhaust rattle and the fender clearance, the drive down was nearly flawless, but there was still the trip to the BMW CCA Foundation for the opening of the Passion exhibit, the drive to Hot Springs for The Vintage event itself, and the return drive home. So I wasn't popping the champagne (or stowing the antifreeze) just yet.

The Wegweiserization

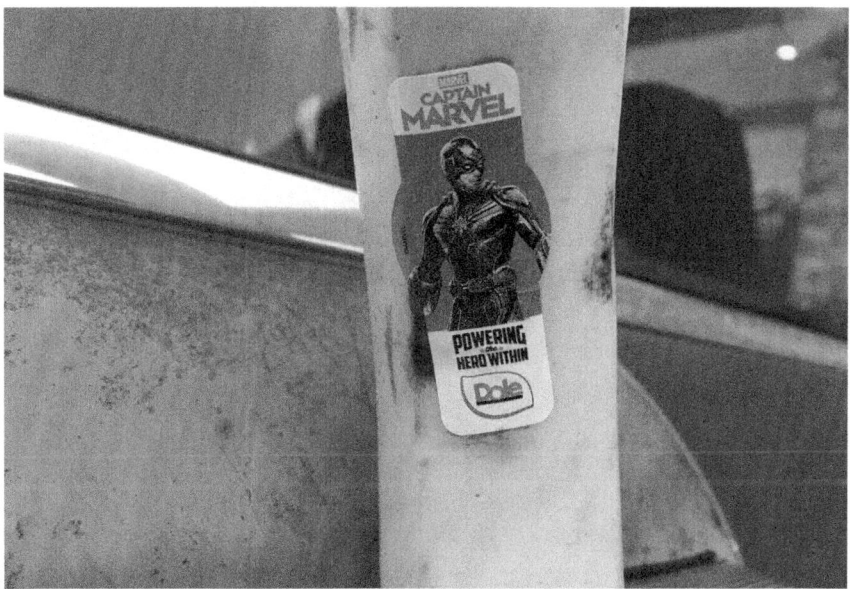

Once Bertha was sitting in the parking lot at The Clarion Inn, the Vintage's event hotel, something happened. It was, uh, unique.

It began with the banana.

You have to understand that there's a five-year history of my friend Paul Wegweiser playing pranks on me at The Vintage. In 2014, I brought the Sahara-colored Bavaria I'd just purchased. If I recall correctly, Paul took exception to the color. I awoke the next morning to find a hand-painted "BRF-ARIA" license plate attached to the car. But as the day progressed, photos began showing up on Facebook of a guy dressed up in a chicken suit, appearing to perform—I'm not quite sure how to say this—an unnatural act with the car. To this day, Paul denies it was him. I've learned to take these things at face value. *Someone* was dressed in a chicken suit and doing bizarre things to my car. Of that I can be certain.

Figure 151: The Vintage, 2014. Not sure what it was about the Bavaria that brought the worst out in Paul. Or even if this was Paul. (photo by Brad Day)

Figure 152: Uh, yeah. (photo by Brad Day)

The following year, Paul expanded on the chicken-related theme and, during the dead of night, inundated my Bavaria with yellow feathers, plastic eggs, and Mardi Gras–themed swag. The video of the aftermath can be seen by searching YouTube for "Rob Siegel Paul Wegweiser Bavaria chicken episode." (Well, what the hell would *you* have labeled it?) I'm still pulling feathers out of the car's crevices.

Figure 153: The 2015 feathering of the Bavaria.

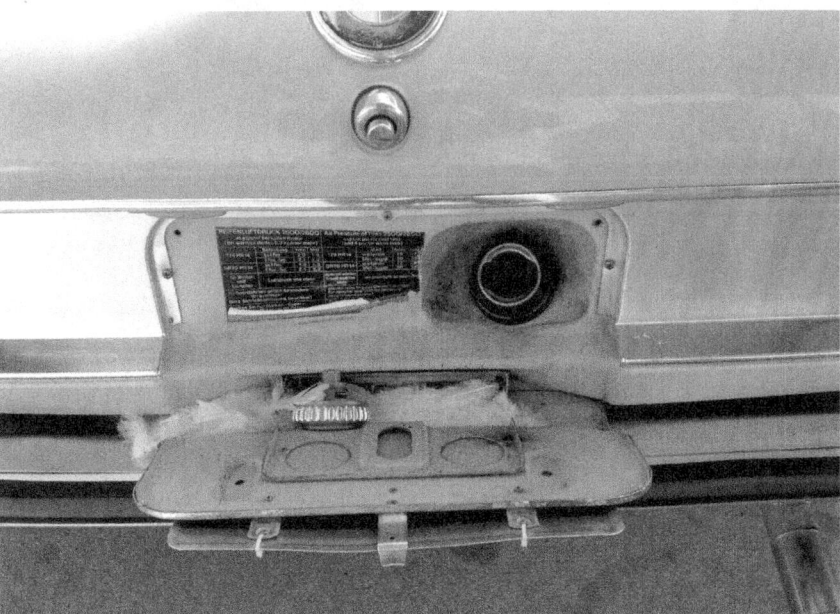

Figure 154: Found these during my first fill-up on the drive home. They're still there. I never had the heart to remove them.

Then, in 2017, I caught Paul red-handed installing a license plate surround on Louie that claimed certain provocative things about the relationship between my income and my, uh, manhood (what it said was "I may be broke but I have a HUGE PENIS"). He intentionally mounted it upside down because that way it was, you know, subtle.

Figure 155: Busted. Photo by Brad Day.

Why does Paul do these things? I have no idea (seriously, I really don't), but it's become part of the event. Some Vintage attendees regard it as performance art. To our Facebook friends, it's a spectator sport.

In 2018, Paul had Hodgkin's lymphoma and missed The Vintage. I drove down in my Euro '79 635CSi. Nothing Wegweiser happened to the car. That is, until after I arrived home. When I went back to the garage to unpack the car, I noticed a single yellow feather under the accelerator pedal. I went inside and bellowed at Maire Anne and Ethan: *"WHICH ONE OF YOU IS RESPONSIBLE FOR THIS?"* They both claimed innocence. I believed them, because I'm a trusting idiot. My wife never lies to me, though my son I'm not sure about. At the time, I shrugged and assumed that a feather must've drifted out of something

I'd packed (there are, after all, still feathers that I've never had the heart to remove in the back of the multimeter). It was only during the writing of this piece, a year later, that my dear sweet wife admitted that she had been less than truthful with me, and that Paul had put her up to it. Yes, I was remotely Wegweisered. *By my wife*. With friends like that, who needs a lying spouse?

Figure 156: Last year, Paul had his evil minions taunt me remotely. I only recently learned that those minions were my wife.

Paul has since recovered, and he confided in me before the trip that this meant that he'd had *two years* to think how he was going to "get me." It was clear that Bertha and I were in for a first-rate full-on Wegweisering.

So, when, the morning after my first night's stay at the Clarion, I came out to my car to find this, I knew that it had begun.

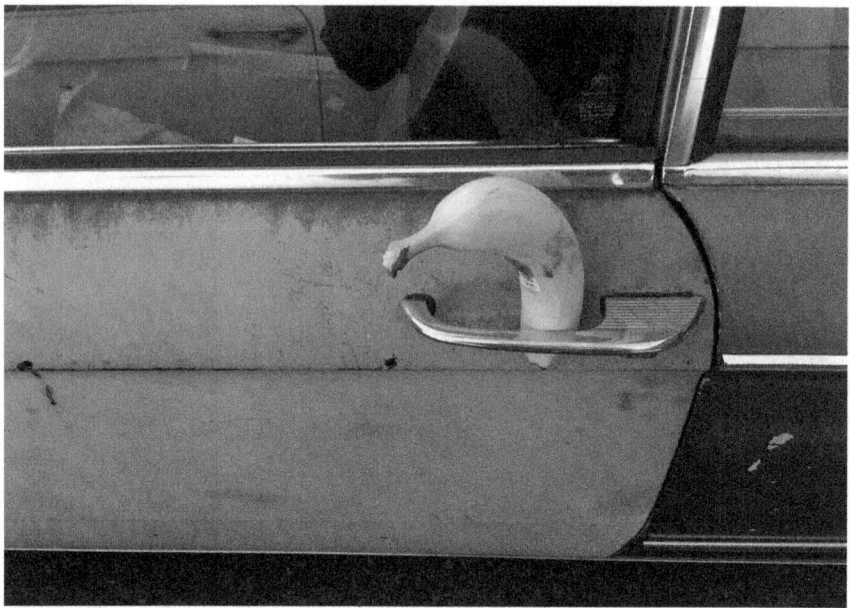

Figure 157: The Wegweiser equivalent of putting the horse head in the bed.

When these things happen, I've learned to channel my best *Animal House* Dean Wormer, shake my fist at the sky, and scream, with increasing pitch, *"WEGWEISER!"* But I had no clue what it meant, or that it had portent in terms of a larger prank.

The next day, unbeknownst to me, Paul conspired with our mutual friends, giving many of them bananas and asking them to nonchalantly eat them while walking or driving past me. I was in the parking lot of the BMW CCA Foundation at the "Passion" exhibit with Jim and Susan Strickland, the people who'd bought The Lama (they actually drove it to The Vintage) when Vintage organizers Brad Day and his wife Anne Marie Vincent drove slowly past me in their Turkis 2002. Susan gently said "Uh, Rob," and pointed. I looked up in time to catch Anne Marie doing a slow-motion drive-by banana eating. It may have been the single funniest food-related thing I have ever seen, but again, I had no idea what it meant.

Figure 158: Well, what would you think this meant?

On the drive back from the Foundation, the weather was swelteringly hot, and Bertha's passenger cabin began to absolutely stink of fuel. I thought that the plastic fuel line that runs inside the car (which I'd just pressed into service prior to this trip) had split. So that evening, I went out to the parking lot to see if I could address the fuel smell. I noticed that Paul was parked practically next to Bertha, but didn't think anything of it (I can be focused to the point of stupidity). I took the car for a one-exit romp on the highway and didn't smell anything, making split-plastic-line theory unlikely. When I got back, Paul and I pored over it, and he noticed that there was an unplugged hole on the rubber fuel filler neck.

"Yeah," I said, "I meant to run a vent line for that. But I doubt that's the source of the smell. I drove all the way down that way and it was fine."

"But it was bitchin' hot today," Paul said. "There must've been a lot more vapor in the tank. That was probably the difference." I decided that he probably was right. I found a length of line, ran it from the port to outside the car to vent the tank, and thanked Paul for his expertise.

Then, it was immediately back to monkey business. "Don't even bother to lock it," Paul suddenly said. "I've got like 20 2002 keys with me. One of them will fit. And if not, I'll be inside it with a coat hanger in thirty seconds."

I locked it.

It didn't matter.

The next morning, I ran into my friend Clay Weiland at breakfast. It turned out that, on the drive back from the Foundation, he experienced overheating problems in his 2800 E3 due to the brakes binding up. He'd managed to get his hands on some caliper rebuild kits and was about to go out and put things back together. I offered my help, and he accepted.

I went out to Bertha to swing her next to Clay's car, and encountered my Wegweiser-related fate. I deeply regret that in my haste to help Clay, I didn't capture the scene with a walk-around video the way I did with the Bavaria episode, but here are some stills. Note how my antenna has been turned into, I don't know what, perhaps a net for catching very small gorillas.

Figure 159: This photo doesn't fully convey the number of bananas that were on or around my car.

Figure 160: A roundel with hand-painted banana. I actually really like this bit of detail on Bertha.

Figure 161: This shows the copious quantities of gorilla hair adorning my front seat. And the lovely note saying "Sorry that stuff got a little weird. Your ape pal, Georgo and Mindy." And a nozzle. Because... I really have no idea.

Figure 162: One of four bunches of bananas found inside the car. There were others placed UNDER THE WHEEL WELLS.

Figure 163: Because who DOESN'T want fake hibiscus hanging from their sunroof crank?

Figure 164: If you can't make this lettering out, it says "Party ape wagon-o-rama."

Figure 165: Yes, Bertha's right side window reads "Apelovin' get freaky."

Figure 166: The piece de resistance.

I cleared enough of the freaky ape-lovin party-o-rama-related swag away to be able to drive the car over next to Clay's, and spent the next hour and a half helping him reinstall the brake calipers in his E3. Unfortunately, we were not able to successfully bleed them; it appeared that one channel of the master cylinder had become non-functional. (I should note that Clay's problem was pretty unusual. Brake pads can certainly wear down until you hear metal on metal, and on long downhills, it's possible for brakes to overheat and fade, but it's really pretty rare for brakes to go from functional to non-functional and strand you in a vintage car, which is why I don't include them in "The Big Seven.")

As the clock swung past 10:15 am, I told Clay that, since I was on the hook to cover The Vintage for *Roundel* magazine, I needed to, you know, actually *be* there, and left him in the hands of other capable help, including professional mechanic Le Tran.

Figure 167: Clay Weiland trying to dig himself out from under his E3's brake problems.

Since I left late for Hot Springs (where the actual Saturday Vintage event is held, about an hour north of the Clarion), I missed much of the BMW traffic and largely had the twisty roads to myself, which was great, though I was keenly aware of the potential rubbing of Bertha's right rear tire every time I hit a good left-hander at speed. But the entire drive up, the gorilla mask, which was sitting between the shift lever and the glove box, kept glowering up at me.

As I approached the turnoff to the Hot Springs event field, I realized: *I had to drive into the event wearing the mask.* I had no choice. It was my destiny. I came to a full stop in traffic, put my foot firmly on the brake so I wouldn't rear-end the E30 in front of me, and attempted to put the mask on. It was a very snug fit, and the mask's cheek bone jabbed me right in the eye. I pulled it off, and closed the gap that had opened up in traffic in front of me. I tried a second time, and the same thing happened—right in the eye. If it was my destiny, it wasn't going well.

By this time, I was perhaps one car length from the turn in. Now or never. I tried one last time. This time the mask's eye sockets aligned perfectly with mine. I thought, okay, we're totally doing this, and made a right turn into the event field. By utter chance, event Festmeister Scott Sturdy was at the head of the driveway. He looked at me, I turned my head directly toward him, did my best New Jersey "*What?*" and drove in.

Figure 168: Wegweiser started it. I was just finishing it. (Photo by Brad Day)

I noticed that, in the back seat of the E30 I followed in while wearing the mask, there were two small children. As I drove across the field, I kept thinking "Turn *around!* Turn *around!* There's a guy behind you driving a car while wearing a gorilla mask! It's *funny!*" Eventually one of them did, and I got to see her elbow her sister, and then the wide-eyed expression when *she* turned around. After we both parked and I took off the mask, I introduced myself to the girls and their parents. Their mother, Stephanie Smithwick, was the owner of the E30. Obviously I needed to explain to her the context of the mask and all the gorilla-related crap in my car, which led to the subject of Paul and the history of his pranking me. She listened intently as I explained the context that led up to this insanity.

"And *why* does Paul do this?" she asked, so reasonably and non-judgmentally that it made me briefly realize how seriously fucked up the whole thing must sound.

"Really, I have no idea."

"And what do you do to get him back?"

I thought for a moment. "Nothing," I said. "Absolutely nothing."

"That must be completely unnerving to him."

"Well, I bloody well hope so."

As Stephanie and I talked, I learned that she actually knows Paul, at least by phone, because the E30 is hers and she orders parts from Paul. She then explained, without a hint of bravado, that after she bought the E30, she tucked the bumpers, dropped the rear subframe, and changed the bushings. The more she talked, the more I realized she was a total badass masquerading as a young mother with a slight Maryland lilt in her voice. I wound up writing a *Roundel* magazine column about her titled "Car Girl" that opened with the line "When I met Stephanie Smithwick and her E30 at The Vintage, I was wearing a gorilla mask. And her story is *still* much better than mine."

Shortly after, I had the pleasure of seeing and hanging out for a bit with my friend Alan Hunter Johansson, he who gave me the Cibié Oscar driving lights that were adorning Bertha's bumper.

Figure 169: Alan Hunter Johansson and me posing with the Cibiés.

I then tried to balance my journalistic duties with simply being a car guy enjoying the event. That rhythm, however, was soon interrupted by what became, for me, the most significant part of the trip.

TIMELINE

1975
July 8: Manufactured in Munich, West Germany
July 17: Delivered to BMW NA

1984
May 10th: Purchased by me in Austin, Texas
June: Swapped in freshly rebuilt motor from my other 2002
August: Moved up to Boston
August 31: Drove Bertha off from our wedding

1986
March: Second engine rebuild with 10:1 pistons, Iskenderian 300 degree cam, and sidedraft Weber 40DCOEs
June: Installation of Koni suspension

1987
July: Third engine rebuild due to ruined crankshaft
September: Road trip to Nova Scotia

1988
August: Loaned to Alex and Heidi for their honeymoon western road trip
September: Sold to Alex

1990
Stolen and recovered
Installed 5-speed

1991
Stolen and recovered with damage
Put into storage

2018

May 28: "Sell me back Bertha. Do it. *Do it! DO IT!*"

May 30: Verbal agreement

June 2: Oh dear god what did I do?

June 10: Bertha driven out of her tomb and towed home

July 8: Up and running but nowhere near ready to drive to Oktoberfest

July 17: First drive around the block

July 18: First nail and wail

July 21: Registered!

August 6: Windshield replaced and car inspected!

September 12: Differential replaced, driveline rumble and whine gone

September 19: Mini road trip to Rhode Island Cars & Burgers

October 6: Bumper swap completed

December 9: Out in Fitchburg for the winter

2000   2005   2010   2015   2020

Bertha sleeps for 26 yearzzzzzzzzzzzzzz

2019

April 29: Back from Fitchburg

May: Vintage Prep

May 15: Off to The Vintage

May 16: The Wegweisering

May 20: Home again

September: *Resurrecting Bertha* book published

Banana Cream Pie

1 baked pie crust, 9"
3 tbsp cornstarch
1⅔ cups water
14 oz sweetened condensed milk
3 egg yolks, beaten
2 tsp butter
1 tsp vanilla extract
3 bananas
lemon juice
whipped cream

In saucepan, dissolve cornstarch in water; stir in sweetened condensed milk and egg yolks. Cook and stir until thickened and bubbly.

Remove from heat; add butter and vanilla. Cool slightly.

Slice 2 bananas; dip in lemon juice and drain. Arrange on bottom of prepared crust. Pour filling over bananas; cover. Chill 4 hours or until set.

Spread top with whipped cream. Slice remaining banana; dip in lemon juice, drain, and garnish top of pie.

Repairing the World, One Giubo at a Time

You might not think you could top the gorilla-and-banana-related events as the central pillar of The Vintage 2019. But for me, the giubo episode had a deeper and richer meaning. And it wasn't even Bertha's giubo.

I wasn't at the event for fifteen minutes when someone told me that my hack wrenching services were required. I was introduced to Jeff Rose, who had driven his mint-green 2002 down from Delaware for his first Vintage. Jeff said that about 15 miles from Hot Springs, he heard a loud *BANG!* and saw pieces fly out behind the car. He said that after that, the shifter was very loose and he heard a lot of metallic noise from the transmission. (I later asked Jeff how he knew to hunt me down. He said that he went to the BMW CCA tent, described what had happened to his car, and was told "Find either Rob Siegel or Paul Wegweiser. One of them will help you." Our destinies are written in ways we are not always aware of.)

I tried to crawl under Jeff's car, but it was too low. I could, however, get one shoulder under and reach up with my arm. I was able to move the back of the shift platform laterally left and right by several inches, from which it appeared likely that one of the platform bushings was detached from the rear of the transmission.

But after I extricated myself, professional mechanic Reggie Stewart suggested that perhaps the transmission noise might be a bad giubo. I again put my shoulder and arm under as far as I could, reached up to lay my hand on the giubo, and was astonished at what I felt: The giubo appeared to have completely disintegrated. All I felt were the flanges, bolts and nuts, no rubber giubo pieces at all.

Figure 170: Trying to use my hands as my eyes and diagnose Jeff's car. (photo by Reggie Stewart)

I advised Jeff that he couldn't drive it the 50-ish miles back to Asheville, much less back to Delaware, this way without risking damaging the transmission and driveshaft flanges. I said that I had a spare giubo (the one I'd brought in case Bertha's distorted one self-destructed) and a small floor jack, but unfortunately, as I said above, this was the first long road trip I'd taken without bringing jack stands. So I offered that, if we found jack stands and a solid surface on which to set the car, I'd fix it for him, but since I was covering the event for *Roundel* magazine, it'd need to be at the end of the day, after the festivities were over. Jeff said that he'd met a guy, a fellow who was selling a ratty rusty white '68 2002 at the vendor area, who said he lived nearby and offered a space where we could work.

I found the gentleman, an interesting Porsche guy in his early 70s named Nort Northam. He confirmed that he lived just a stone's throw away, and had a small barn with a cement floor. Unfortunately, he had no jack stands, but even still, a hard floor and a roof sounded great, as it was beastly hot on the Hot Springs field, and we did need a safe surface on which to use the floor jack.

For the rest of the day at The Vintage, I alternated between doing my journalistic duties and asking people if they had jack stands. To my surprise, I kept striking out. While I was out making these excursions, Susan and Jim Strickland hung out at my car, rewarding people with beer if they bought my books. After the third sortie, I came back empty-handed and obviously disappointed.

"What are you looking for again?" Jim Strickland asked me.

"Jack stands," I said. "I can't fix Jeff's car without them."

"*That's* what you're looking for?" Jim laughed. "I have a set in the trunk of The Lama."

"*You... have... jack... stands... in... The Lama?*"

"Yes," Jim said. "You told me to buy them as part of your road-trip recommendations."

Well then. We walked over to my former E28, Jim pulled the brand-new jack stands out of the trunk, and I deposited them in Jeff's mint-green 2002.

When the event ended a bit after five, we limped Jeff's car over to Nort's barn. It was easy to find, as the ratty white 2002 we'd seen for sale was in the driveway. Jeff backed his car in, I jacked it up with my little floor jack, set it on the stands, and had at it.

Figure 171: Jeff's mint-green 2002 in Nort Northam's barn, with Bertha's trunk disgorging tools. (photo by Jeff Rose)

Figure 172: My little floor jack was just enough to set the car on the newly-procured jack stands. (photo by Jeff Rose)

When I crawled under the car and looked at the giubo, I was astonished a second time. It was present and intact. A few of the bolts were loose, but I had no idea what I'd laid my hands on when I'd reached under that made me think the entire giubo was missing. It was bizarre.

So I set about repairing the loose shift platform. Jeff had found someone selling the bushings and Allen-head bolts that hold them in. The bushings on the back of the transmission were fine, but the platform was loose because one of the bolts had fallen out. I installed the one Jeff had bought, and made sure the other one was tight.

That just left tightening up the giubo bolts. To reach them all, I needed to jack up the back of the car so I could rotate the driveshaft, and with it, the giubo. As I spun the giubo around, I had my third giubo-related surprise: I saw that the entire top quarter was completely missing. This was how I'd gotten it wrong. Apparently, by chance, when I'd reached up under the car to feel the giubo, I'd put my hand into the area where the chunk was missing, and laid it on a bare bolt. It was possible that the platform bolt came out, got lodged in the rotating giubo, and tore it up. Jeff was lucky that it hadn't broken the transmission flange.

Figure 173: I've seen worse.

Replacing a giubo isn't a big deal—remove the three nuts and bolts to separate the exhaust resonator from the headpipe, undo the two nuts holding on the center support bearing, remove four of the giubo bolts, lower the front of the driveshaft, undo the other four giubo bolts, install new part, reassemble—but after being in the hot sun all day, I was burned, dehydrated, and tired, and it was all I could do to finish the job. But no bolts were rusty or seized, and the work went along quickly enough.

When I finished, Jeff was incredibly grateful, and talked about paying me, but I demurred. I was about to launch into a lengthy explanation about how often I've been the recipient of grace and generosity, but just then, Nort interrupted me and simply said: "It's called pay-it-forward. It's just how we do it. Next time, *you* help someone." It was true, concise, and beautiful.

Figure 174: (Left to right) yours truly, Jeff Rose, and Nort Northam.

Jeff and I later swapped messages in which I asked him exactly how he'd connected with Nort. "He found *me*," Jeff said. "He was walking around the field, saw my car, said that his first 911 was the same mint-green color, we started talking, I told him about the problem, and he offered his space." When you couple that with the combination of serendipity and resourcefulness with which Jeff had found me, it's pretty amazing.

If I may digress for a moment, I guess I should explain the roots of my behavior. I am neither a boy scout nor the CVS Good Samaritan (google it). In truth, for much of my life, I was more sinner than saint, and in many ways, I'm an innately selfish person. But I am other things as well, and one of them is a lapsed Jew raised by a single mother who spent her life being kind and generous to other people. She successfully instilled in me the importance of and the joy in performing mitzvot. If you look up the word, the primary meaning is "commandments," a list of 613 things you should do and not do in order to "be Jewish." This, of course, ruffles my iconoclast atheist feathers, and from that description, I can think of few things that I would have less interest in. However, the secondary meaning of mitzvot, and the way my mother has always used it, is "good deeds." (My son Ethan once brilliantly referred to my mother as "the Ted Williams of mitzvah hitting.") The concept of "tikkun olam," which means "repair the world," and which was discussed during my mother's version of the Passover Seder, is something that also sunk in. If, out of everything in my upbringing, I've taken these two lessons, let them bake, and regurgitated them as the need to fix strangers' broken cars, so be it. ("The Hack Mechanic: Repairing the world, one giubo at a time.")

Look. I have been the recipient of much grace and generosity in my life (the major theme of my book *Ran When Parked* is about how the resurrection and road trip of Louie was enabled by the kindness of strangers or near-strangers), but this is about more than just paying it forward. We have control over so few things in life. I can't eliminate hatred, or hunger, or homelessness, or stop the warming of the planet, or fix health care, but I could fix this guy's giubo. I felt good, he was grateful, everybody wins. For a brief and perfect moment, I'd repaired both of our worlds. Honestly, what could be better? Try it sometime.

In the final flawless capping of the giubo episode, I checked back later that evening with Jeff to make sure he'd returned the jack stands to Jim and Susan. Jeff said they told him to keep them, that that was their deposit in the pay-it-forward bank. Perfect.

So, thanks ma.

Can you understand why the giubo episode was my favorite part of the whole trip?

Wrapping Up the Road Trip

Photo by Brian Ach.

The drive back from Nort's barn to the hotel was absolute heaven. Bertha and I had performed our mitzvah, and this was our reward. I nailed and wailed, snapping the car through the tight switchbacks heading up out of Hot Springs, and through the long sweepers as the road widened, the rubbing right rear tire be damned. Some of this cavalier behavior may have been from fatigue, maybe a touch of heatstroke, but in that moment, mostly it was a simple "fuck it," the risk/reward dial turned to the eleven setting of reward. The car coming on the cam, the Webers roaring deep throaty and metallic, wailing *WAAAAAAAAAAAAH blip waahhhhhhhhhhhh…* it was so glorious that it almost made me sad for the overwhelming segment of humanity that has never experienced such ecstasy as that which can result behind the wheel of a vintage car with a hot engine and a tight suspension. *This* is what these cars are for. *This* is why I do this. It's not to have the car sit in a garage or win a fucking trophy. It's *this*. As Jon Stewart used to say, here it is, your moment of Zen. At least it was for me.

Exhausted, parched, and hungry, I arrived back at the hotel and texted my friends, who had no idea where I'd been for the last several hours. Fortunately they were at a restaurant a stone's throw away. I went in, sat next to Paul, and drained a beer.

"You know," he said, "I loved that not only weren't you mad at me, but that you embraced all the gorilla-related craziness. You not only embraced it, you *owned* it."

I thought about it for about ten seconds, then said "You really have no idea what you've done."

Paul looked at me. "You're right," he said, "because I have no idea where you're going with this."

"This drive down with Bertha," I explained, "was not just to get down here—I mean, I had to drive down in *something*—but also to provide the ending for the new book. After her resurrection, Bertha needed a road trip. Yes, she deserved a road trip after being cooped up for 26 years, but more than that, her *story* needed a road trip. But a road trip needs drama. That worked great with Louie in *Ran When Parked*, because, as you know, that car really *did* make it home by the skin of its teeth. But Bertha's drive down was pretty uneventful. There were no breakdowns. No repairs by the side of the interstate. Nothing even close. Granted, we haven't gotten back home yet, so I might be jinxing myself, but at this rate, the drive home will be similar. That's great, but there's not a lot of drama in it. Perhaps I prepped her too well. "Nothing broke" makes for a lousy story.

"So, what you did with your opening up a can of Wegweiser on Bertha, you crazy fuck, was so much better than my academic notion that the book needs a road trip and a road trip needs drama. By going full-on Bertha the way you did, you, uh, got some on her. You welcomed her into The Vintage fold in a special and intimate way that's far better and far more meaningful than anything I could've ever imagined. So thank you. For the bananas and all that other weird shit. Really."

Paul gave me a big hug.

"But you're still a dick," I said.

My friend Brian Ach joined Andrew, Jose and I for the drive back. This was a joy, as there's a whole story of my fixing Brian's 2002tii after it did not successfully make it down to The Vintage in 2015 (the cause turned out to be a broken spring in one of the fuel injectors, which no one else I know, not even the pros, has ever seen). So every time since then that Brian has driven the car down to The Vintage and back, it's like a triumph of determinism, a reassurance that mechanical systems can be fixed and be relied on, a thumb in the eye of bad juju. We all accompanied Andrew back to the dealership to pick up his repaired M5.

The two-day drive home *did* occur without incident. Well, almost. My air conditioning blower fan switched on and off several times, then failed altogether. When I checked the fuses, I found that one of them had melted. If you look carefully at the photo below, you can see that the metal part of the fuse is actually intact, but the body of the fuse is a cheap plastic aftermarket replacement (the original ones are ceramic, not plastic), and the plastic melted. I replaced it with a ceramic one and had no trouble on the rest of the trip. I posted the photo on Facebook, and got the usual sarcastic comments about substituting a gum wrapper, a penny, or a .22 caliber shell.

Figure 175: One of these things is not like the others.

So. 1966 miles. One exhaust rattle, one rubbing tire, one unplugged gas tank vent line, and one melted fuse. A per-tank high of 27.5 mpg, and a low of 17.2, the latter of which was when I was nailing and wailing through the twisties on the way back and forth to Hot Springs. The average fuel economy was 24.1. Oh, and the car did not use a drop of oil. From an engine with a 300 degree reground cam and Weber 40DCOEs that were jetted in 1985, and a bottom end that wasn't touched. Incredible.

Yes, they're just cars, but buying back Bertha—the car Maire Anne and I drove off from our wedding in in 1984—resurrecting it, taking it on a trip like this, having it behave so magnificently, and having it welcomed into The Vintage fold in this special intimate way, made for an amazing year. Even though both the car and I were bone-tired from the trip, we were both grinning like idiots.

After I got home, I received a message from Paul regarding the burned-out fuse. "You know," he said, "when I was putting bananas in your car, I *thought* I smelled burned wiring up under the dash. Better check carefully." I did, and was horrified when I found several wires that had burned clear through their insulation.

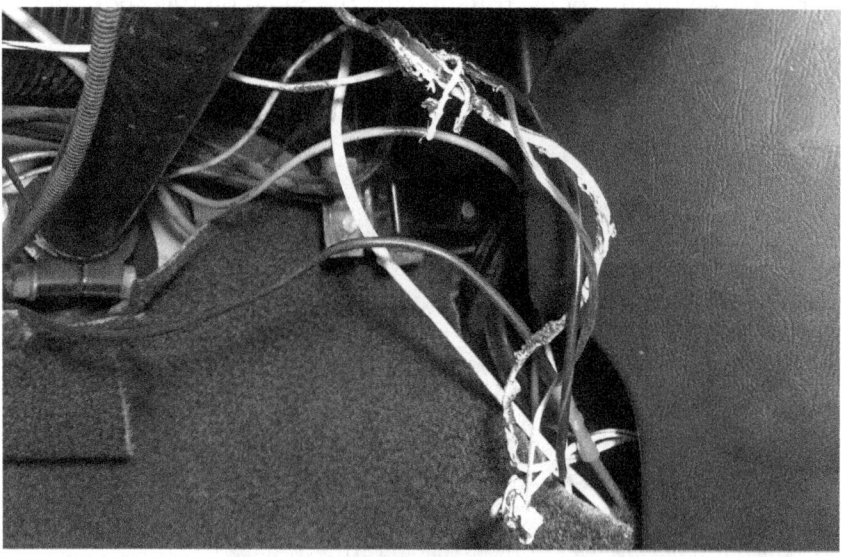

Figure 176: Toasted wires. Way not good.

Geez, I thought; I guess that fuse incident really *did* do some damage.

However, upon closer examination, I found that none of the wires went anywhere; they were simply held in place by a zip tie.

WEGWEISER!!

Epilogue

The day after I got back from The Vintage, I got a call from my landlord in Fitchburg telling me that there was an issue with the lock on one of the spaces I rent. It turned out to be nothing, but it gave me a reason to go out there and swap cars—put Bertha away for a while and let her rest after her 2000-mile banana-soaked adventure, and give one of the other cars some quality time.

Before I headed for Fitchburg, I put Bertha on the lift and fixed the exhaust rattle (the headpipe hitting the unobtanium Metric Mechanic 5-speed support bracket) that had spooked me on the trip down. As I said earlier, the bracket isn't really adjustable, but I loosened the bolts that hold it on the back of the transmission, and there was just enough play in the bolt holes to shove the trani, and with it, the engine and the attached headpipe, up maybe an eighth of an inch and stop the rattling.

Then I de-Wegweisered Bertha, reverently putting all of the gorilla-related accouterments, including the mask, in a plastic bag, and placing it carefully in the trunk. Well, not *all* of them. I left the roundel with the hand-painted banana where Paul had placed it in the middle of the speedometer. It's Bertha's Vintage T-shirt. It'll live there forever. And the hair that hangs from the glove box. Can't get rid of *that*, at least not yet.

But the "ape- party-o-rama" lettering... I can't drive around Newton with *that*, right? It has to go. I took a single-edged razor blade and was about to scrape it off when... I just couldn't. I left it on, thinking how happy it'll make me when I retrieve the car from Fitchburg and see it still on there. It does need to come off, I thought, but not today.

It occurred to me that all of these things are like the bad soul patch, the questionable tattoo, and the broken heart you picked up that summer in Amsterdam. Your parents and friends are on you to clean up and move on, but you're just not quite ready.

I then drove Bertha out to Fitchburg, and was instantly reminded how dangerously fun the car is when she's not hauling 500 pounds of tools and books.

As I said earlier, part of Bertha's ethos and my emotional bond with the car is that she can't be Jessie from *Toy Story*—abandoned, locked away for decades, then rescued but still terrified of being put back into storage. As I parked Bertha in one of the garage spaces in Fitchburg and rolled the door down, I decided to quit worrying about it. She'll never be abandoned again. I know that now. She's just too much fun.

And the whole question of the car's usage envelope (finding that balance between locking her away so she doesn't rust versus not caring if she does)? I quit worrying about that too. *Our* aging doesn't stop. Neither does that of our loved ones. Why should it with our cars? I hope we live a long and happy life together before we're both put in the ground.

This is not a car that made it home from The Vintage by the skin of its teeth. This is a car that's at the beginning of her new adventures. If she's Jessie, then I'm just a big kid who's never going to grow up.

(Addendum: My wife just told me that, prior to The Vintage, Paul tried to get her to send him a set of keys to Bertha. She said no. It's almost enough to make me forgive her for that damn feather.)

My Mother Totally Deserves The Last Word

Photo by Kenneth Siegel.

As the Bertha-Vintage trip approached in May 2019, even though my mother appeared to be stable after her eight-day hospital stay in April, I wasn't entirely comfortable leaving. I asked her, and she simply said "*GO!*" Not long after I returned, however, it became clear how serious things were. I saw her just about every day for the last six weeks of her life. I finished writing the book a few weeks before she entered hospice care, and had the chance to read her the chapter on "Repairing the World, One Giubo at a Time." Not surprisingly, she loved it. What mother, Jewish or otherwise, wouldn't love hearing that she was instrumental in making her son a mensch, and that her son not only knows it, but publicly gives her credit for it?

On July 12th 2019, my remarkable mother, Bernice Siegel, the kindest, most generous, most rational, most empathetic, and all-around best person I've ever met or ever *will* meet, passed away.

Among the many things my mother gave me was the best bit of parenting advice ever. She said: "If your child shows interest or passion in something, treat that like a flower, because if you don't, you'll kill it with neglect, or worse." My car passion kicked into gear when I was an adult, so I can't directly credit her with allowing it to blossom. But I can and do credit her with my realizing that, even in adulthood, passion should be treated like a flower, and that *you yourself are responsible for not killing your own passion through neglect or worse*. So, the questionable purchases, the ridiculous projects, the foolish road trips, and the great memories from all of them... ma, it's all you.

But if there's an afterlife, could you drive something more interesting than a Toyota Corolla? You're making me look bad.

(You can read my eulogy to my mother at thehackmechanic.blogspot.com.)

End Notes

Rob Siegel has been writing the monthly column *The Hack Mechanic*™ for BMW CCA *Roundel* magazine for over 30 years. He is the author of the books *Memoirs of a Hack Mechanic, The Hack Mechanic*™ *Guide to European Automotive Electrical Systems*, and *Mechanical Ignition Handbook: The Hack Mechanic*™ *Guide to Vintage Ignition Systems*, all from Bentley Publishers, and *Ran When Parked: How I Resurrected a Decade-Dead 1972 BMW 2002tii a Thousand Miles Back Home, and How You Can, Too*, and *Just Needs a Recharge: The Hack Mechanic*™ *Guide to Vintage Air Conditioning*, all from Hack Mechanic Press. Rob lives in West Newton, Massachusetts with his saint-like wife Maire Anne Diamond, three black cats, one black dog, a roomful of his wife's insects (don't ask; okay, ask, then go to www.bugworks.net), and as many cars and guitars as he can get away with. Given his druthers, he'd rather be a full-time singer/songwriter, but it's more fun to continue to play the part of The Hack Mechanic. Rob says "Most days, I actually am that guy, but really, it's just fucking exhausting being me."

Photo by Aaron Siegel.

Other books by Rob Siegel

Memoirs of a Hack Mechanic: How Fixing Broken BMWs Helped Make Me Whole
(a memoir with actual useful stuff)
Bentley Publishers, 2013
ISBN 978-0837617206

The Hack Mechanic™ Guide to European Electrical Systems
Bentley Publishers, 2013
ISBN 978-0837617510

Mechanical Ignition Handbook: The Hack Mechanic™ Guide to Vintage Ignition Systems
Bentley Publishers, 2017
ISBN 978-0837617206

Ran When Parked: How I Resurrected a Decade-Dead 1972 BMW 2002tii and Road-Tripped it a Thousand Miles Back Home, and How You Can, Too
Hack Mechanic Press, 2017
ISBN 978-0837617671

Just Needs a Recharge: The Hack Mechanic™ Guide to Vintage Air Conditioning
Hack Mechanic Press, 2018
ISBN 978-0998950716

Made in the USA
Middletown, DE
04 June 2023

32045698R00156